THE STORY OF
STONEHENGE

THE STORY OF
STONEHENGE

PATRICIA
SOUTHERN

AMBERLEY

This edition first published 2014

Amberley Publishing
The Hill, Stroud
Gloucestershire, GL5 4EP

www.amberley-books.com

Copyright © Patricia Southern, 2012, 2014

The right of Patricia Southern to be identified
as the Author of this work has been asserted in
accordance with the Copyrights, Designs and
Patents Act 1988.

ISBN 978 1 4456 1900 2

British Library Cataloguing in Publication Data.
A catalogue record for this book is available
from the British Library.

Typesetting and Origination by Amberley Publishing.
Printed in the UK.

CONTENTS

I

INTRODUCTION

Situated on Salisbury Plain in chalk country, Stonehenge is one of the most famous monuments in the world, instantly recognisable in photographs, drawings and plans, and the subject of scholarly study for the past 400 years. And yet, despite all the attention that has been devoted to Stonehenge there are still more questions than answers, and more theories than facts. No one can say with any certainty why it was built, or what it meant to generations of people of the New Stone Age (Neolithic) era. These people built it, used it, abandoned it, and rebuilt it a few times, over many centuries. Each successive group of people may have used the monument for slightly different purposes, perhaps linked by a common shared mythology handed down over the generations. When the Neolithic era gradually segued into the Bronze Age over the centuries, metal tools and weapons eventually took the place of the earlier stone versions. During this long process, prehistoric society changed, and the beliefs and traditions of the Neolithic people were subsumed by new ways of doing things. Stonehenge was finally abandoned and nearly forgotten.

The monument that is visible today is only the last of the transformations that took place on the site. First there was a roughly circular ditch flanked by two banks of earth, one inside the ditch and a smaller one outside it. Then timber structures were erected inside the circle, traceable now only through the post holes that were discovered during excavations in the early twentieth century in the ground between the inner chalk bank and the Sarsen Stone circle. Even the Sarsen Circle was a secondary stone phase, preceded by a simpler Bluestone version that may or may not have been a complete circle. These different versions of Stonehenge had a long history, starting *c.* 3000 BC in the Neolithic era and finally going out of use in the Bronze Age, *c.* 1500 BC. From just a cursory glance at the composite plan of all the phases of the monument, showing everything that had ever been built on the site, it can be quickly and clearly discerned that the life-story of Stonehenge is complex. Only the last phases of its development are visible now, but the full plan includes not only the existing stones, but also the holes where stones once stood in arrangements that differ from the current one. Added to these there are the post holes where wooden posts had been erected, inside and outside the encircling bank and ditch, and then dismantled, or left to decay, before subsequent building began.

All the modern terminology that is used nowadays to describe the various component parts of Stonehenge has been invented by antiquarians who took an interest in the monument from the seventeenth century onwards. They could see only the finished version of Stonehenge, and interpreted it to the best of their ability, without the accumulation of knowledge about prehistoric Britain derived from archaeology, and without the technology for dating that is available nowadays. One of these antiquarians, John

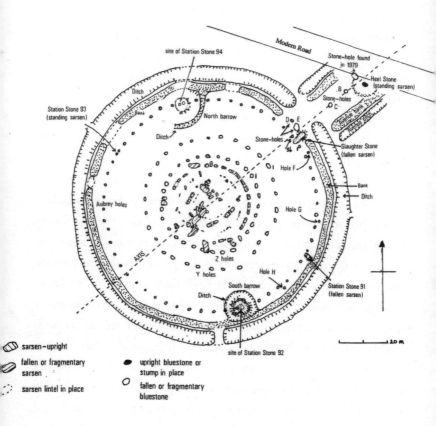

Fig. 1. Composite plan showing most of the visible or excavated features of Stonehenge, except for the so-called Q and R holes of the Double Bluestone Circle which was obliterated when the Sarsen Circle and the five sets of Trilithons were erected. The immensely long history of Stonehenge with its different phases made it difficult for antiquarians and archaeologists to sort out which features were contemporary with others, or which preceded them or post-dated them. The exact dating and chronology of the various phases are still disputed. Only where a stone was raised or a hole was dug cutting into another feature is it possible to say which came first and which second. The complexity of this plan is testament to the vast amount of scholarship that has been devoted to the study and interpretation of Stonehenge from the seventeenth century onwards. Drawn by Jacqui Taylor.

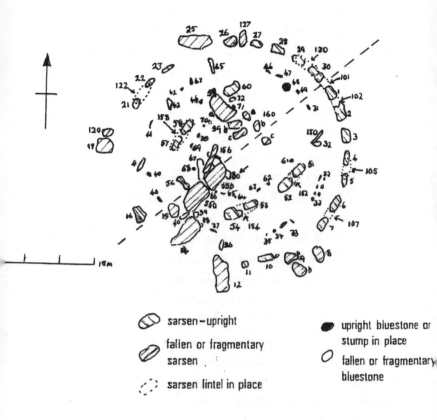

Fig. 2. A more detailed plan of the central area of Stonehenge showing the state of the Sarsen Circle, the Trilithon Horseshoe, and the later Bluestone Circle and Horseshoe. Flinders Petrie, the archaeologist famous for his work on ancient Egypt, established the numbering system for the stones, which involved an analysis of the whole monument to discern which stones among the jumbled mass belonged to the various components of Stonehenge. All sequences of numbers begin at the north-east entrance and run clockwise, starting with the Sarsen Circle, numbered 1 to 30. Drawn by Jacqui Taylor after Darvill 2007.

Aubrey, was ahead of his time. He noticed not only the stones but also discovered the places where holes had been dug and then filled up, although little use was made of his observations until the early twentieth century. From then onwards, archaeologists discovered yet more hidden features of the monument, and started to label and number the existing and vanished stones, and the post holes that were revealed by excavation.

The numbering system for the various stones was begun by Professor Flinders Petrie, who surveyed the monument in 1877. His scheme was continued by later archaeologists, who added further labels as more features came to light that Petrie could not have known about at the end of the nineteenth century. Numbering the stones involves a preliminary identification of which stones from among the jumbled mass of fragments and fallen stones belong to which circuits. Petrie started with the Sarsen Circle, numbering the upright stones and their lintels, beginning at the right-hand side of the north-east entrance as seen from inside the circle, and moving round clockwise. The circle is incomplete now, but numbers were allocated to stones which are no longer there, theorising that on grounds of the regularity of spacing the absent stones once belonged to the original layout, together with their lintels. Broken stones are allocated one single number and its fragments are distinguished by the letters a, b, c, and so on. All numbering sequences for the various features of the Stonehenge circle follow this pattern, starting at the north-east entrance and proceeding in a clockwise direction. The Sarsens of the main circle are numbered 1 to 30, and their matching lintels are given the same denominations increased by one hundred, so it is clear which uprights they belong to. The smaller Bluestones inside this circle are numbered 31 to 49. Inside the circle larger Sarsens are arranged in the form of a horseshoe, formed by five separate pairs of uprights, each pair topped by its own lintel, called Trilithons, a term invented by the antiquarian William Stukeley, meaning 'three stones'. These are numbered 51 to 60, with lintels taking their numbers from the large number of each pair, so they are allocated numbers 152, 154, 156, 158 and 160. Inside the Trilithon Horseshoe, the accompanying Bluestone Horseshoe takes up numbers 61 to 72. The Altar Stone inside the Trilithon Horseshoe is number 80. Numbers 91 to 97 refer to individual stones outside the stone circle, the Heel Stone being number 96, and the Slaughter Stone, now lying flat just inside the bank and ditch, is number 95. This makes it so much easier to be clear about which particular stones are under discussion. Apart from the stones, there are three sequences of holes discovered by excavation, some of which are marked on the ground. Around the circumference, just inside the bank of earth there are fifty-six Aubrey Holes, each currently marked by a white circle in the ground, not necessarily conspicuous, since the main focus for visitors is the stone circle. Inside the monument there were two further sets of paired holes, made at different dates. One set of paired holes was discovered by excavation, and none are visible now because they predated the Sarsen Circle and were obliterated when it was built. This series of holes was given the letters Q and R. A second set of paired holes, dug much later than the Q and R holes, surrounded the Sarsen Circle, and were labelled Y and Z holes. Each of these holes was further distinguished by its own number, such as Q3 or Z5 and so on.

In addition to the numbered sequence of stones, all the different phases of the monument have been allocated numbers. The first scheme was devised by Richard Atkinson, who carried out excavations at the monument in the 1950s and 1960s, and published his important work, simply called *Stonehenge*, in 1956. He thought that the first phase comprised the circular bank and ditch, the Aubrey Holes and the Heel Stone, followed by a second phase when the Avenue was built leading out from the north-east entrance, which was widened to accommodate it, and the stones were set up in the holes labelled Q and R in the centre of the circle. The major third phase was thought to have included the building of the Sarsen Circle and the Trilithon Horseshoe inside it, and the digging of the two circuits of holes, labelled Y and Z, around the outside of the Sarsens. In the last part of this phase, Atkinson thought that the smaller Bluestones were placed inside the Sarsen Circle and the Trilithon Horseshoe. Subsequently, in the light of more evidence, and the development of more sophisticated dating techniques, the chronology of these phases has been revised. Dating techniques include dendrochronology, which utilises the annual growth layer of trees to pinpoint dates when timber was felled, and radiocarbon dating, which measures the decay of carbon-14 in bones and wood (see Dating techniques in the Glossary).

The results of the long-term excavation and modern investigations of the finds at Stonehenge have been assembled and evaluated in a major work published by English Heritage in 1995. This large book, nearly 700 pages, gathers together all the results of excavations since the beginning of the twentieth century: *Stonehenge in its Landscape: twentieth-century excavations*, edited by Rosamund Cleal, K. E. Walker, and Rebecca Montague. Atkinson's proposed sequences for the building the monument have been slightly re-ordered, for instance the Y and Z holes are now thought to belong to the final phase, which was established some considerable time after a long period of disuse of the monument.

According to the revised scheme put forward in the 1995 publication, the earliest phases of Stonehenge are numbered 1 to 2, while the third and most complicated phase, encompassing the final versions of Stonehenge, has been subdivided and presented as 3i, 3ii and so on up to 3vi. In several books these phases are denoted on plans and in the text, but in this book the numbering of the phases is not used, to avoid complication and the necessity to refer to the plans each time a phase is cited by a number. Also the dates and the chronology of the phases are still disputed and may one day be revised. In the text of this book, the various phases are described in sequence, according to their probable chronology, without applying numbers to the sequences. It cannot be emphasised too strongly that the chronology of the various parts of Stonehenge is not yet immutable and probably never will be, and there is hardly any statement about the monument that is immune from dispute, apart from the two ascertainable facts that it is in Wiltshire and it is unique.

The name Stonehenge derives from the Anglo-Saxons who named the hanging stones (*Stan Hengcen*), usually taken to mean the horizontal stones supported by the Sarsens, as if hanging in the air. Some archaeologists and historians prefer to see the name as a reference to what might have happened to human victims, the 'hanging' bit of the name referring to summary justice or perhaps lynching. From the 1930s onwards the latter part of the name Stonehenge has been appropriated to describe timber and stone circles all over the country, which are now known as 'henge' monuments, the irony being that Stonehenge itself breaks all the rules for henge monuments, which are usually defined by an inner ditch and an exterior bank, whereas these features are reversed at Stonehenge, where the ditch is outside the bank. This is not the only anomaly. Stonehenge is unique in many respects.

In addition to the several physical versions of Stonehenge, there is the latest one, the Stonehenge of popular imagination, engendered originally by antiquarians, who examined the monument and attributed grisly purposes to Stonehenge as a whole, and in particular to parts of it, naming them accordingly. A stone that had fallen down near the north-east entrance was thought to have been deliberately set there in its recumbent position especially for the slaughtering of sacrificial victims, and was accordingly labelled the Slaughter Stone (number 95). It is doubtful if anyone or anything was ever slaughtered there, especially as the Slaughter Stone was not always horizontal. Similarly, it is unlikely that sacrificial victims were despatched to the next world on the so-called Altar Stone (number 80), visible now inside the Trilithon Horseshoe in the centre of the monument. These names for individual stones are too deeply embedded in modern consciousness to be eradicated, and there is no need to change them, since the names do serve to distinguish each stone from all the others, and they merit initial capitals when reference is made to them.

Probably the most famous named stone is the Heel Stone (number 96), standing outside the circle and perhaps pre-dating the very first phase. This stone has been given many different names in the past, but Heel Stone is the one that is currently used. Some writers prefer the spelling Hele Stone, and have attempted to find links with Greek *helios* and Celtic *heol*, or *haul* in Welsh, meaning the sun. This is related to the erroneous assumption that the Heel Stone marks the exact position of the midsummer sunrise, a phenomenon which can be demonstrated in wonderfully atmospheric photographs, showing the globe of the rising sun neatly aligned with the top of the Heel Stone. Splendid as these images are, they are fabrications. Anyone can stand some distance behind the Heel Stone and line it up with the rising sun by ignoring one of the two criteria for observing the midsummer sunrise at Stonehenge, which require a marker of some sort and also an established point from which to make the sighting. From the centre of Stonehenge, the midsummer sun rises between the Heel Stone and its now vanished companion stone (number 97), which stood to its left as observed from inside the monument. In the earliest phases of Stonehenge the Heel Stone may have been associated with the moon, marking the midpoint between the most extreme points where the moon rose. In a later phase, the alignment of the whole monument was changed slightly, allowing for a more accurate observation of the midsummer sunrise, and then the Heel Stone and its lost partner could be used for sightings from the centre of Stonehenge.

Another misconception fostered by the antiquarians, who had little to go on except relatively recent British history and the works of the Roman authors, is the supposed use of Stonehenge by the Druids. The monument was ancient history by the time the Druids came to prominence in Britain and Gaul, and there is no evidence that they converted it to a cult site or were ever associated with it. Nevertheless, the image of Druids at work at Stonehenge is indelibly imprinted on modern minds and is recreated at midsummer. None of this does any harm. Purists may scoff at people who get up at an ungodly hour in the middle of June to stand and watch the horizon, while photographers shuffle about until the rising sun does actually sit picturesquely on top of the Heel Stone. It is a mystical experience in its way, and all the scoffing in the world will never answer the question 'what was Stonehenge for?' It is quite possible that even the ancient Britons, who used the site long after it was first marked out, shared similar misconceptions about what their remote ancestors did there, but instead they may have substituted rituals and beliefs of their own, which gave them considerable satisfaction, just as modern people do. Each visitor can construe Stonehenge as he or she wishes, and the enormous interest in the monument from visitors from all over the world will at least ensure that it will be looked after, with no possibility that its stones should be broken up to provide the foundation for a new motorway.

2

BEFORE STONEHENGE: THE MESOLITHIC TO THE EARLY NEOLITHIC, *c.* 8000 BC TO *c.* 3000 BC

The early Neolithic people who created the first Stonehenge did not enter a completely empty landscape and decide to create a monument on the site. The whole surrounding area had been utilised if not occupied for thousands of years, though the only evidence so far uncovered for very ancient activity close to Stonehenge derives from post holes that came to light when the car park was being extended in the 1960s. There were three or possibly four post holes, aligned west to east, though the outermost hole towards the west has also been interpreted not as a post hole, but as a cavity made in ancient times by an uprooted tree. In the 1980s another post hole was discovered further east, though it is not certain if it belonged to the same group. The car park post holes once held wooden posts made of pine, perhaps fashioned rather like totem poles, carved and painted. The dating analysis of the remains showed that the posts were raised at some time between 8500 BC and 6500 BC, not very precise perhaps, but startling enough, because it places the totem poles firmly in the Mesolithic era, or Middle Stone Age which preceded the Neolithic era. Oak and other trees that are common nowadays had not yet been established in Mesolithic Britain, which explains why the then freely available pine was used for the poles. The wide range of dating evidence for the poles may indicate that each one was raised in succession, possibly after the preceding poles had rotted away, rather than being raised all at the same time.

Archaeologists distinguish between prehistoric peoples by the kind of tools and weapons they used, since there is nothing else to work with, no historical records, no interpretable language, no personal names. Before the introduction of metals, stone tools were used for an extremely long period, which is divided up by archaeologists and historians into three convenient groups, based on changes in the type of tools used. The term 'Mesolithic' translates as Middle Stone Age, utilising ancient Greek words: *meso* means middle, and the 'lithic' element derives from the Greek for stone, while Palaeolithic refers to the very remote past, labelled in English the Old Stone Age. Neolithic means the New Stone Age. During this long period of many centuries, the way of life changed from reliance upon hunting and gathering, and the consequent mobility of the groups of people, to a more settled life based on stock raising and farming. This is an abbreviated description which conceals an enormously long time span and a great deal of debate.

Since Mesolithic people depended on hunting and gathering they moved around after the animals that they hunted, perhaps responding to seasonal variations for gathering wild food. They left only scant trace of themselves at their temporary settlement sites, but their way of life was successful enough to support a population that evidently expanded, and there is accumulating evidence that they were not as primitive or as rootless as was once thought. Typical finds on a Mesolithic site consist of tiny, deliberately shaped flints designed for fairly sophisticated weapons, such as arrowheads. These are labelled by modern archaeologists as microliths, meaning 'small stones', as opposed to megaliths, meaning large stones. 'Megalithic' is a term that is applied to monuments all over the world where enormous stones were set up for various purposes, for instance at Stonehenge itself. It does not denote a specific time frame in the same way that the terms Mesolithic and Neolithic are used.

The small flint tools and weapons of the Mesolithic era are the most significant indicators of the activities of people, but not necessarily of settlement sites. However, as archaeological techniques continue to improve, archaeologists have discovered subtle evidence that might once have gone unnoticed, such as signs of post holes for wooden supports which are starting to emerge on Mesolithic sites, interpreted as temporary dwellings. An important Mesolithic site has been excavated for several years at Star Carr in Yorkshire, yielding much evidence about how the people lived. It was probably not a permanently occupied site, but one to which groups of people continually returned.

Unfortunately, apart from the so-called totem poles found in the extension to the car park, there are, as yet, no further signs of Mesolithic activity in the area of Stonehenge, though the fact that poles were erected may indicate that the site of Stonehenge had specific meaning to Mesolithic groups. It is thought that there may have been an ongoing tradition about the site that survived from the Mesolithic into Neolithic times. Perhaps the whole area around what would become Stonehenge was considered sacred, possibly relating to an ancestor cult.

The early Neolithic landscape

The Neolithic era, starting around 4500 BC, saw the introduction of farming, perhaps first by domesticating animals, and then by crop growing. There was probably no abrupt change, but a meld of two different lifestyles, called 'acculturation' by archaeologists, that lasted for centuries. The late Mesolithic and the early Neolithic people probably combined hunting and gathering with a more settled means of obtaining food.

Although lifestyles perhaps did not change fundamentally or rapidly, some of the changes that occurred in the Neolithic area are highly visible. Pottery appears for the first time, as far back as the fifth millennium BC. One of the most visible changes from the Mesolithic to the Neolithic is discernible in the impact that the Neolithic people had on the landscape. Around the Stonehenge area, as indeed all over the country, signs that communities had settled and established farms have to be sought for by excavation, but the monuments that appeared during the Neolithic era were massive and many of them are still visible. These comprise causewayed enclosures, earthen long barrows and cursus monuments, all names invented by archaeologists for a series of features that display considerable diversity within each group.

Causewayed enclosures

Causewayed enclosures are found all over Britain, with concentrations in the south, though this may simply reflect the archaeological work that has been done in identifying them. There may be others lurking undetected in other parts of the country, perhaps ploughed out over the centuries, or simply not yet noticed in the landscape. Several causewayed enclosures have been distinguished by aerial photography, but only a few have been excavated. Perhaps the most famous, and also possibly the largest,

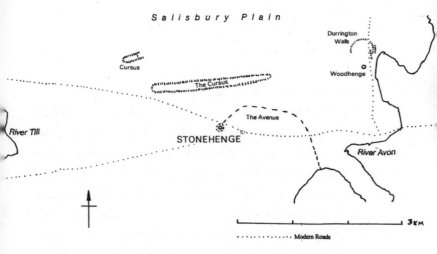

Fig. 3. Plan of the Stonehenge area showing some of the major prehistoric monuments. These were not all in use at the same time. The Cursus predates Stonehenge, and the Avenue was a later addition to the monument. The area around Stonehenge contains many burial mounds, not shown on this plan, consisting of earthen long barrows, which may have gone out of use by the time the first phase of Stonehenge was built, and round barrows, some of which were contemporary with the monument. The henge at Durrington Walls is interpreted as the place where the Stonehenge people lived, using the river Avon to convey the remains of their dead to the place of the ancestors at Stonehenge. Drawn by Jacqui Taylor.

is Windmill Hill near Avebury, where there are three concentric ditches with causeways across them, surrounding a hilltop site with good views all around. Windmill Hill has become the type site for causewayed enclosures, and has been excavated and studied for several seasons.

The causewayed enclosures were once called causewayed camps, because when they were first recognised it seemed that they must have been settlements with defences around them, similar to the much later hill forts of the Iron Age. The definition was complicated by the fact that at a later stage in their development some of these causewayed enclosures *were* defended. Perhaps the only ones which were turned into defended enclosures were those which were already conveniently sited on hills which could be easily fortified, such as Crickley Hill in Gloucestershire, founded on a high limestone ridge with natural advantages for defence. In converting the sites, in some cases the ditches were made deeper, and probably palisades were added to the banks. It seemed to early archaeologists that the causewayed enclosures must have been all the same and that they had been erected with purely defensive purposes in mind. But the theory that these were all defended enclosures had to be discarded when more and more causewayed enclosures were discovered, and it became clear that they all had multiple entrances across the ditches, making defence difficult or well-nigh impossible. For a while, the name changed to 'interrupted ditch enclosures', which explains the structures much more clearly, though nowadays the term causewayed enclosure is used to describe this category of Neolithic monument.

The enclosures vary tremendously in size, but they share the common features of a roughly circular area defined by an internal bank of earth accompanied by an external ditch. The construction of all Neolithic ditches involved digging short straight sections, which in the case of causewayed enclosures were not joined up, so there was access across the uncut earth between the individual segments of the ditch, giving rise to the title 'causewayed enclosure', The prime purpose of each enclosure cannot have been to keep people or animals out, nor was it to keep livestock inside it, unless fences were erected over each and every causeway, which would have been labour-intensive. In any case there is no evidence of post holes for fences across the causeways.

If the reason for building such enclosures was to keep people and animals out, or to keep livestock inside the circuit, it would have completely unnecessary to make fences if only the several causeways across the banks and ditches had been removed except at a couple of points, a scheme that cannot have escaped the minds of the Neolithic population, therefore different purposes other than use as stockades or corrals must be sought. The finds from these enclosures are so diverse that it is concluded that the enclosed areas were used for several different purposes, but not for continuous habitation. At Windmill Hill no irrefutable houses were found, but there were signs that people had stayed there for continuous periods, probably for feasts and ceremonies. There were large amounts of pottery which was not native to the local area, so it may have been used as a centre for exchange of goods, either as trade and commerce, or gift exchange ceremonies between local and neighbouring peoples, or possibly both functions at the same time. Stone axes may have been traded or exchanged here as well, the finer ones for ceremonial functions and prestige gifts, the less fine ones traded as tools.

Deliberate deposits of animal bones with butcher marks on them, and fairly frequent discoveries of the remains of hazelnuts, might indicate feasting and seasonal ceremonials, but among the finds in causewayed enclosures there are also flint tools, objects made of chalk that probably represent male and female genitalia, and buried human bones. There may have been fertility cult festivals, possibly in conjunction with celebrations at planting time and harvest, and also associations with death and an ancestor cult, all enacted within the causewayed enclosures, as well as other uses which we cannot distinguish at a remove of several thousand years. There was a causewayed enclosure a short distance to the north-west of Stonehenge, called Robin Hood's Ball, with two sets of ditches. It had gone out of use by the time the first monument at Stonehenge was built and there is very little to see on the ground after centuries of ploughing have obliterated it. Though there was some overlap with henge monuments, most other causewayed enclosures had either been abandoned or were nearly at the end of their lives when the first Stonehenge was constructed. So far there is no evidence that causewayed enclosures were still used after the middle of the third millennium BC. It has been suggested that in some places the henge monuments replaced the causewayed enclosures, though the reason why a new kind of site should be established and the old ones should be abandoned remains unclear.

Long barrows

Another class of Neolithic monument, prominent in the landscape, is the earthen long barrow, where the bones of the dead were installed. These were built from about 3800 BC and went out of use probably 600 years later. Around the Stonehenge area, there are several barrows, mostly oriented to the east, though not all of them follow this pattern. Since only a few of the barrows have been excavated it is not known what is inside the majority of them, but on analogy with those that have been investigated, it can be assumed that they consist of huge mounds of earth with a ditch on either side, trapezoidal in shape and higher at one end than the other, so the barrows taper downwards to a narrow end. The broader end usually consists of an entranceway, perhaps fenced off from the rest of the barrow, where some sort of funeral ceremonies may have been held while the mortuary chambers were still open and not yet sealed in earth. Some completed barrows have prominent 'horns' on either side of the entrance, flanking an area like a small courtyard. A good example is Belas Knap in Gloucestershire.

The earth mounds usually cover timber-lined or stone-built mortuary chambers where the bones of the dead were interred. The large stones or wooden partitions framed individual chambers, usually on either side of a passageway between them. These were not like graves, where inhumations of whole bodies took place. Instead the mortuary chambers held collections of bones from corpses which had gone through a process of de-fleshing, the technical term for which is excarnation. This would have been achieved either by exposure to the elements at some sacred place until only the bones remained, or by deliberate removal of the flesh. Such practices were possibly carried out in the entranceway to the barrow, often called a forecourt, which usually was fenced off from the chambers. Bones and skeletal fragments have been found in these forecourt areas at some barrows.

When de-fleshing was complete, the bones were then placed inside the mortuary chambers, often jumbled up without regard to the individuals to whom they had belonged. It seems that on occasion the bones were sorted and rearranged within the chambers. Though it is usually possible to say how many different individuals are represented by the jumbled collections of bones, it is rare that complete skeletons can be reconstructed because many bones are missing. Emphasis seems to have been placed on the long bones, and possibly skulls, though in one case there are several more lower jaws than there are matching skulls.

The mortuary chambers may have been left open for some considerable time, possibly for several centuries, until it was decided to cover them over and build the barrow, which sealed the tomb and its contents. The size of the barrows, some of them up to 100 metres long, was totally out of proportion to the chambers themselves, which occupy only a small part of the burial mounds. These practices indicate beliefs and rituals far removed from modern ideology about death, perhaps deriving from the need to free the spirit entirely from the body before the dead could be regarded as really dead, and thus finally removed from the realms of the living. Some modern archaeologists interpret the Neolithic landscape in terms of zones of the dead, belonging to the ancestors, and zones of the living where the ceremonials were carried out and the settlements were developed, though these two functions were not necessarily placed at exactly the same sites.

By the time when the first Stonehenge was built, the long barrows were going out of use, and the communal burials of the bones of the ancestors were starting to give way to individual burials. In Scotland and Wales, communal burials persisted for longer but in England cremation became more fashionable, instead of exposing the body until the flesh had disappeared. At Stonehenge there are many deposits of cremated bones, so it is interpreted as a cremation cemetery, at least in its early phases.

The full significance of the change from the use of communal burial mounds to individual burials and cremations cannot be assessed. The belief that the spirits of the ancestors could not be freed until the body had disappeared was probably still upheld, but cremation would hasten the process, and the fact that the ashes and the bones were carefully buried suggests that the same reverence as before was still accorded to the person represented by the remains. The cremated bone fragments were usually gathered into a leather bag, with the edges held together by a bone or wooden pin.

Cursus monuments

The so-called Great and Lesser Cursus monuments to the north of Stonehenge belong to another class of earthwork of the Neolithic period. The Great Cursus is an elongated rectangle oriented east to west, 1.86 miles (3 kilometres) in length and about 490 feet (150 metres) wide, defined by two parallel internal banks and flanking ditches, and squared off at both ends. The Lesser Cursus lies to the north-west of this much larger monument. There are many other similar cursus monuments in Britain, the longest so far discovered being the Dorset Cursus, running for over 6 miles (10 kilometres) straight across the country uphill and down dale without regard to the features of the landscape. Cursus monuments vary greatly in size and have no rigidly uniform style, some being very short, others longer, some having open ends and others having a bank and ditch to close off one or both ends. They may have served different purposes, but perhaps not the one suggested by William Stukeley, who first noticed the Great Cursus at Stonehenge in the eighteenth century. Having nothing to compare it with except the circuses of the Roman Empire, he thought that it must have been used for races. At least he noticed it and described it, and no one can prove categorically that his ideas are wrong. It is just that it feels wrong.

The elongated shape of the Great Cursus does suggest some sort of processional way, but for a procession all that is needed is a marked path with a starting point and an end point. The effort of digging two ditches and erecting two banks of earth for 3 kilometres ought to indicate something more elaborate. It is noted that some cursus monuments are aimed at rivers, and the Great Cursus north of Stonehenge runs eastwards to the River Avon (the Wiltshire one, not the Stratford one or any of the other Avons), with a standing stone between the terminus and the river, though the full significance of this is not established. The east to west orientation would allow people inside the Great Cursus to observe the sunrise at the March equinox, and the sunset at the September equinox, but there is no evidence to show that Neolithic people were interested in the equinoctial sunrise and sunset, and not all cursus monuments are oriented in this way to allow for the same observations.

There may have been a belief that the east represented rebirth, which may explain why several barrows around Stonehenge were oriented towards the east. The Great Cursus may have had a connection with death and rebirth, as some archaeologists have suggested. In this case the banks of earth and the ditches of the Great Cursus would have divided the realm of the dead from the realm of the living. The first Stonehenge may have had similar attributes. Dating evidence for the Great Cursus is problematic since finds that could be tested by radiocarbon dating techniques may have been deposited long after the construction of the monument. Although there is considerable variation in suggested dates for the Great Cursus, it does seem that it was established several centuries before 3000 BC and may have been still in use when the first Stonehenge was built.

3

THE FIRST STONEHENGE,
c. 3100 BC TO *c.* 2550 BC

The Neolithic people had already made an impact on the
Stonehenge landscape before attention was turned to the main site
itself. Around 3100 or 3000 BC, a circular ditch and bank was
created in the middle of the Salisbury Plain. The turf was stripped
off to dig the ditch through the chalk. The circuit was perhaps
marked out by planting a stake in the centre and using a long rope
to swing round like a compass point to delineate the place where
the ditch should be. A small bank of earth was thrown up outside
the ditch, and a much larger one was built inside it. These features,
much worn down, can still be seen today, surrounding the Sarsen
Stones. They are turf-covered now, but when freshly dug in the
chalk they would probably have been spectacularly white, visible
for some considerable distance. There were two entrances into the
circle across the bank and ditch, one in the north-east, and another
smaller one in the south. There may have been a third gap to the
south-west, but usually modern plans show only two, in the south
and north-east.

The bank and ditch arrangement at Stonehenge is more
reminiscent of the causewayed enclosures than the accepted form

of henge monuments, where the ditch is usually *inside* the bank. It is possible that the original intention was to establish a causewayed enclosure, but if so it may have been somewhat anachronistic since most causewayed enclosures seem to have been going out of use around this time.

The circular ditch was not dug out as a continuous circle, but in common with other Neolithic ditches, especially those at causewayed enclosures, the Stonehenge ditch was created in a series of straight sections, but unlike other causewayed enclosures the sections were not interrupted by causeways where the chalk was left intact. The sections of the Stonehenge ditch were all joined up by knocking down the edges where they touched, though this usually left slight protrusions jutting out from the sides of the ditch. Some plans of Stonehenge are detailed enough to show this feature, and the appearance has been compared to a string of sausages laid out in a circle. The individual sections may have been assigned to a team of diggers, possibly even a family group.

The bank inside the ditch has not received a great deal of attention from archaeologists but one sector was investigated and it was revealed that a line of post holes ran along the ground underneath the centre of the bank. It is suggested that the first Stonehenge may have been enclosed by a wooden palisade before the ditch and bank appeared. This hypothetical palisade may have been removed when the bank was built, but it is also possible that that the chalk earth was piled up around the posts, which perhaps protruded above the bank to provide a fence, but all this rests purely on speculation.

There are several other features which may belong to the first version of Stonehenge, some of which may predate the bank and ditch, while others may be contemporary, or even belong to a later phase. No one can be certain about dating, since the material from various parts of the ditch, and from some of the post holes that have been found, may represent later deposits placed there some time after the feature in question had been created. The dating process simply dates the artefacts, not the date when the digging was done. It is rare that finds can be categorically described as primary.

The Heel Stone

One feature that may predate the circle is the Heel Stone, probably originally set up with other stones arranged in lines to mark a route, and in this way indicating a place of great importance in remote antiquity. The Heel Stone now leans towards the ditch and bank of the north-east entrance. Perhaps significantly, the Heel Stone was never dressed and deliberately shaped like the upright Sarsen Stones of the later monument. This factor need not indicate that the stone predates the circular bank and ditch, but it might mean that it was venerated in its original state, and it may have been one of the reasons why Stonehenge was built in this location. During some stage of the development of Stonehenge, the Heel Stone had a close companion on its northern flank, but this stone was removed at an unknown date, for an unknown reason.

Posts at the north-east entrance: a solar and lunar observatory?

The main entrance to the monument at Stonehenge was from the very first oriented towards the north-east, where the sun rises in midsummer. This may have been a coincidence, but many scholars argue that it was a deliberate choice, and since the north–east entrance was never altered in subsequent phases of

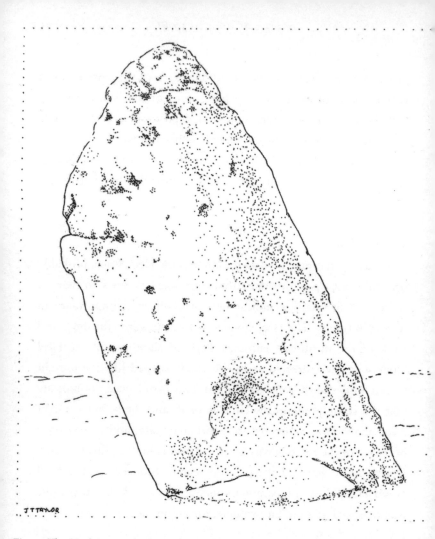

Fig. 4. The Heel Stone, the latest label for this stone of many names, is associated in popular tradition with the midsummer sunrise. It is a Sarsen Stone like those of uprights of the Circle and Trilithon Horseshoe, but it was probably set up hundreds of years before the stone circle was planned, perhaps even before the first phase of the bank and ditch was dug. The stone is in its natural state, not smoothed and shaped like the stones of the Circle and Horseshoe. It leans towards the monument but was once proudly upright with a partner stone which has since vanished. These two stones flanked the midsummer sunrise as seen from the centre of the monument, so the rising sun at midsummer does not appear exactly above the Heel Stone, although in the future, after thousands of years have elapsed, it will eventually do so.

Stonehenge, except to make the entrance gap a little wider and to refine the alignment to allow for a more accurate observation of the midsummer sunrise, it would seem that this orientation was important. Prehistoric people may have been just as concerned with the rising of the midsummer sun as modern enthusiasts are nowadays.

Throughout the year, the positions of the sunrise and sunset move gradually along the horizon. In midsummer, when days are long, the sun rises in the north-east and crosses a wide arc of the sky, skirting roughly three quarters of the horizon, to set in the north-west. In midwinter, when days are short, the sun rises in the south-east, traversing only a small sector of the sky and horizon, to set in the south-west. At the rising and setting of the sun in midsummer and midwinter the sun seems to linger for a few days at the extreme points before it starts to move back along the horizon, a small distance each day, as it rises and sets. These extreme points at midsummer and midwinter are called the solstices, which literally translated means that the sun appears to stand still. In midsummer the rising sun appears to linger in the north-east for a few days, though after midsummer's day it is already imperceptibly starting to move back to the east, and the days gradually become shorter.

In modern times, the year begins on 1 January, and there are calendars to tell us what the date is, so we can mark and remember birthdays and other anniversaries. Without these tools, the changing seasons demonstrate the turn of the year, but not very precisely. The onset of winter vaguely points to the end of one year and the start of the next, flourishing vegetation announces spring and summer, and the glorious bronze leaves of deciduous trees mark the onset of autumn. But in this sort of primitive calendar it is not possible to establish a specific date. Only recurring celestial events can elucidate the passage of time with any accuracy. The fixed points of midsummer sunrise and midwinter sunset are predictable, and either of these points can be used to indicate the day when the new annual cycle will begin. This holds good for many centuries, through hundreds of lifetimes, but there is a very gradual progression along the horizon where the midsummer sun rises and sets. In astronomical terms it is known as the ecliptic, and the rate of change is known and measurable. What this means for Stonehenge is that in 3000 BC the midsummer sunrise would have occurred slightly further north than it does now, and further to the left of the Heel Stone, gradually moving a little further along the horizon with each millennium. Attempts have been made in the twentieth century to use this phenomenon to ascertain the date when Stonehenge was built, by calculating the points where the sun would have risen on midsummer day *c.* 3000 BC through to *c.* 1000 BC, but the important factor that remains uncertain is that the point from which observations were made is not known, so neither the alignment or the axis can be established. What is known is that later in the history of Stonehenge the axis was changed slightly, perhaps allowing for a more accurate observation of the midsummer sunrise than was possible in the arrangement of the first version of Stonehenge.

It is possible that the moon was observed at Stonehenge from very early in the history of the monument. Between the Heel Stone and the north-east entrance a row of post holes was discovered, labelled 'A' posts. They run roughly north-west to south-east. Astronomical theories about Stonehenge link these posts to a series of smaller post holes, or more properly stake holes, neatly ensconced within the entrance between the two rounded terminals of the ditches. It has been suggested that these smaller post holes, arranged in six rows, were set up to mark the progression of the moonrise as it approached its northernmost point, possibly used in association with the 'A' posts . The moon, like the sun, rises more or less in the east and sets more or less in the west, but unlike the sun it does not follow a predictable annual cycle.

The moon has a much more complicated cycle than the sun, not only varying in one month between first quarter to full moon to last quarter and then the dark moon, but also rising and setting some 40 minutes later each day. The moon therefore rises at a different time and in a slightly different place each day, and it takes 18.6 years for the moon to complete one full cycle, when it rises and sets in the same place as it did nearly nineteen years previously. This cycle can be marked at any point, but it could be said that when it rises in the extreme north-east, it has ended one cycle and begun another. The six rows of posts in the north-eastern entrance to Stonehenge have been interpreted as markers for the successive stages of the moonrise until the extreme point is reached. The fact that there are six rows may mean that the whole 18.6-year cycle was observed six times and posts were set up each time. If so, this represents a very long-term co-ordinated project that would have to be taught to and handed down to successive generations for more than a century. It seems that the cycles of the moon were still of great importance to the people of Stonehenge after the posts at the north-east entrance were removed, since the Four Station Stones, which are more fully described in the next chapter, were laid out with their sight-lines directed to the midsummer sunrise, and also to the extreme northerly setting of the moon. The extreme points of the moonset as well as the moonrise may well have been observed at the earliest monument at Stonehenge, but up

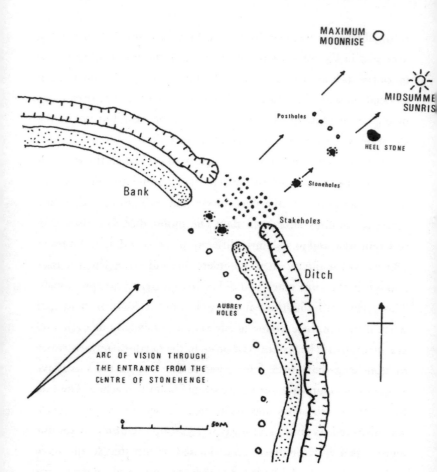

Fig. 5. The earliest version of Stonehenge may have been used as an observatory for the movements of the moon and the sun. The series of post or stake holes across the north-east entrance may have been set up as a means of observing the moon at its most north-easterly position. The moon follows an 18.6 year cycle, so after rising in the extreme north-east, it does not rise at this point again until the 18.6 year period has elapsed. Observation of this north-easterly rising may have been undertaken to mark the end of one cycle and the beginning of another. The four post holes further out from the rows of stake holes may have been connected with the lunar observations, but this is not certain, and would have been more efficient if there had been six posts, only four of which have been definitely attested. More prosaically, the series of stake holes have been interpreted as the remains of a complicated barrier of posts, possibly linked by wattle fencing, shielding the entrance. The larger holes further out from the stakes may have once held totem poles. Drawn by Jacqui Taylor after Burl 1981. Meanwhile, splendid atmospheric photos can be taken with the sun's disc sitting on top of the Heel Stone if the photographer moves away from the site line in the centre of the circle. Drawn by Jacqui Taylor.

to now the only hints that the cycles of the moon may have been monitored concerns the extreme north-easterly rising. The date when the Station Stones were set up is not known, except that they were later than the Aubrey Holes of about 2800 BC (described below) and earlier than the ring of Sarsen Stones of about 2500 or 2450 BC.

If there was any association between the 'A' posts standing further out from the entrance, and the six rows of stakes within it, and if their joint purpose was to observe the most northerly moonrise, it would require at least two more 'A' posts to the north to be able to align the smaller posts with the larger ones to mark the extreme point. If there ever were two extra 'A' posts, at least one of them would have been obliterated when the ditch of the much later Avenue was created, connecting Stonehenge with the River Avon, so there can be no proof that there ever was, or was not, another post or possibly more than one. Another more down to earth alternative is that the 'A' posts were totem poles, like the much earlier Mesolithic examples, now marked out in the car park.

Not all archaeologists agree with the lunar observation theory, preferring to interpret the six rows of posts as fences to block the entrance to the interior of the circular bank and ditch, which presupposes that they were contemporary with the first monument, and that nothing whatever was observed from the north-east entrance. No one can prove or disprove that the Neolithic people of Stonehenge watched the moon or the sun rising and setting, and if they did, the reasons are obscure, but what is certain is that the Salisbury Plain, once it was cleared of trees, is one of the few places where the landscape allows complete observation of the moon and sun around the whole horizon. The midsummer sunrise can be seen directly opposite the midwinter sunset, and vice versa the midwinter sunrise is in direct line with the midsummer sunset. At most other sites, the configuration of the land does not allow observers to see all these phenomena at such perfect right angles, because even a slight rise in the ground alters the level of the horizon, so that the sun seems to rise over the raised land slightly later than it does on the plain, or it goes down slightly earlier if it sets behind a hill, and the alignments of these features will not produce a right angle if marked on the ground. The same principle applies to the observation of the moon at Stonehenge, where views of its rising and setting are more clearly visible than at any other site. For astronomical purposes, Stonehenge is perfect, and it seems that the Neolithic people knew this, and may have set up the first Stonehenge to take advantage of the site.

There may have been festivals even in Mesolithic times connected with the phases of the moon, but these would be impossible to verify. As for Neolithic farmers, there may have been some connection with agricultural processes, much as some gardeners believe that planting should take place at the full moon, but no one needs to go to the bother of setting up six rows of stakes to know when the full moon is about to appear.

Most if not all aspects of prehistoric life were probably imbued with religious or superstitious meaning. On analogy with tribal societies of more recent times, it is highly likely that there was no sharp division between daily life and religious life. The sun and the moon would have been the most likely objects of worship in some form. There may have been a group of people whose task it was to observe the skies and the celestial phenomena. These may have been priests, or even priestesses, who perhaps came from the same family, trained from generation to generation in the rituals involved.

Scientific study for its own sake in Neolithic times is generally dismissed as a valid theory, but among the hypothetical group of observers there may have been one or two individuals with an absorbing fascination with the sun, moon and stars just for the pursuit of knowledge, whether or not the results of the study had any relevance to festivals or religious beliefs. If the moon was a venerated celestial body requiring worship and propitiation, who were the people who started the observations to find out what it actually did, accumulating knowledge empirically over a long period of time, even if the ultimate aim was for religious purposes? Surely curiosity and a search for answers is not a purely modern attribute? Is that not what science is all about? Nobody would suggest nowadays that the various observatories all over the world are connected to religion, but one important point is that modern society is organised so that certain people are freed from the need to use most of their time to grow crops, tend animals, and search for food, and it is possible that in Neolithic times there were a few equally privileged people who were supported by others, so that they could continue with their observations. It may have been important to celebrate certain propitiatory rites to ensure that the moon embarked on its new cycle, but before this kind of ritual could be established, a prerequisite is a series of recurrent observations to provide the knowledge of what the moon could be expected to do at various times. Chicken and egg: which came first, religious fervour followed by investigation and accumulated knowledge, or accumulation of knowledge through observation and then a refinement of religious practices?

The extreme points of sunrises and sunsets may also have been marked with appropriate ceremonial. At Stonehenge the midsummer sunrise is directly opposite the midwinter sunrise, and although the modern focus is on midsummer, there is evidence from other prehistoric sites that midwinter risings and settings of the sun were observed. In Cumbria, at the stone circle known as Long Meg and Her Daughters, the standing stone outside the vast circle, Long Meg herself, is aligned with the midwinter sunset, and perhaps more famously, at the prehistoric tomb of Newgrange in Ireland, the passageway between the burial chambers is illuminated by the midwinter sunrise. This is not accidental. The engineering of the tomb to achieve the phenomenon where the sun strikes and illuminates the very end of the passageway is sophisticated. The sun shines through a roof box at the entrance, where a removable lintel had been installed. At midwinter, this would be taken out to allow the light to shine through. A few minutes after dawn at midwinter, the light begins to shine into the passage and then moves gradually further and further along it. The passage itself had to be sloped to allow the sun's rays to penetrate to the rear, where for a few seconds it lights up the rear side chamber. Even after the tomb had been sealed the roof box could be opened up at the appropriate time and the sun could shine on the domain of the ancestors inside. The focus on midwinter is not limited to Newgrange. The midwinter sunset was obviously considered important by some societies. This is unmistakable in Cumbria, where the stone circle called Long Meg and Her Daughters is oriented to the midwinter sunset, marked by Long Meg herself, the tall standing stone outside the circle.

There is unfortunately no evidence that would enable us to apply the label shamans or priests to any group of people who watched the skies, if such there were, nor is it possible to use any other term with connotations of leadership. If there ever was an individual or a group in charge of the procedures and responsible for the accumulating knowledge gained from observations of the moon and the sun, such a responsibility would be imbued with religious significance. It is possible that each single row of the six rows of posts may represent one full 18.6-year cycle of the moon, which in turn suggests that six successive cycles were observed. This would have been a very long-term co-ordinated project lasting for more than one century, and therefore involving a process of teaching and handing down accumulated knowledge to successive generations. Primitive societies with no written records find other ways of recording events, by incising marks on bone and wood, or tying knots in strings, and the Neolithic inhabitants of the area around Stonehenge would have been just as capable as any other people of memorising what these records meant. In this connection, several bones have been found on other prehistoric sites in different countries, all bearing marks that have been interpreted as records of the phases of the moon.

The Aubrey Holes

Many more post holes besides those at the north-east entrance have been discovered inside the first circle at Stonehenge. Around the perimeter there were fifty-six holes, a few of which were first noticed by the antiquarian John Aubrey when he was surveying the monument for Charles II in 1666. Aubrey had already drawn up a report on the stone circle at Avebury, which he came upon while out hunting in 1649. After the restoration of the monarchy, Aubrey submitted his report to Charles II and in 1663 he accompanied the King to Avebury, and also to Silbury Hill, where the King climbed to the top. Perhaps it was then that the scheme for a survey of Stonehenge was formed.

In the course of his survey, Aubrey claimed that he saw five depressions in the ground, which he concluded must once have

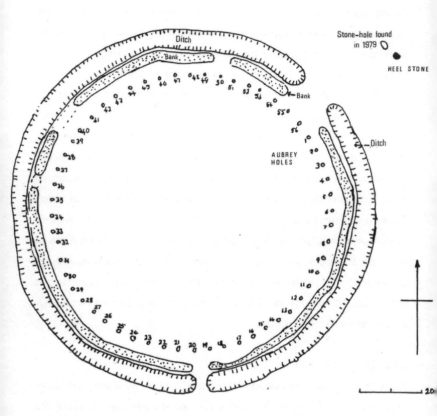

Fig. 6. The first phase of Stonehenge, c.3100 to 3000 BC, consisted of an external ditch excavated from the chalk, and an internal bank formed from the up cast from the ditch. A smaller bank was constructed outside the ditch. There were breaks in both the banks and the ditch in the north-east and in the south. Neolithic ditches were usually dug out with antler picks and shoulder blade shovels in a series of individual trenches, separated from each other by walls of earth, or chalk in the case of Stonehenge, which were then demolished to create the whole circuit. The result, on a large scale plan, resembles a string of sausages. The series of 56 holes, dug from about 2800 BC inside the bank, are named after John Aubrey who discovered a few of them in the seventeenth century. The rest were found during excavations in the twentieth century. They are numbered from 1 to 56, starting at the north-east and following a clockwise circuit. The 56 Aubrey Holes have been linked to the 18.6 year cycles of the moon, and it has been suggested that they could have been used to predict lunar eclipses. One problem with this theory is that the holes may not all have been open at the same time, and there is still controversy over their contents. Without knowing that there was a complete circle of holes, Aubrey thought that those that he found must have held stones. Some modern archaeologists suggest that they held wooden posts. The only certainty is that some of the holes held fragments of bones from cremation burials. Drawn by Jacqui Taylor after Chippindale 1994.

held upright stones. Since the whole of the visible monument in Aubrey's day was constructed of stones, this was a natural conclusion to have made at the time. He was fortunate that he surveyed the area in a very dry summer, when any spot where a hole or ditch had once been dug would show a healthier growth of grass, just as crop marks nowadays can aid modern archaeologists with access to aeroplanes. Crops grow better where there were ditches because the soil there retains moisture, and where walls once stood the crops are deprived of water and therefore growth is stunted and from the air the hidden lines of buried walls look more parched.

Aubrey's records escaped detailed notice until the early twentieth century when archaeologists began to study his observations, and eventually found another fifty-one holes. These fifty-six holes are now called Aubrey Holes, after their discoverer. Many, but not all of them, have been excavated, and from the results it is clear that the Aubrey Holes are not all of uniform size or depth, and the spacing of them is far from regular, though it would require a very large-scale plan to show this irregularity. Nevertheless, the holes are uniform enough to suggest that they were all dug at the same time, and they form as perfect a circle as could be made without using modern surveying equipment. What they were for is another matter.

Some archaeologists in the early twentieth century, followed by some modern scholars today, suggest that the Aubrey Holes held stones. A recent theory is that these stones were Bluestones, which would place the arrival of these controversial stones much earlier than originally thought, before the so-called Double Bluestone Circle was built in the centre of the monument, around 2550 BC. According to this more recent theory, these Bluestones may have been removed from the Aubrey Holes and taken to the bank of the River Avon, where evidence was found that there had been a small Bluestone Circle situated at the end of a passageway leading to the river from the Neolithic henge monument at Durrington Walls, a short distance to the north of Stonehenge. Discussion on these particular points would fill several learned journal articles, so this author, not qualified to pass judgement, intends to move quickly on to the theory that the Aubrey Holes held wooden posts. The evidence for this is circumstantial. Many of the holes contained bone and charcoal, and evidence of cremation burials, so this may have been the prime purpose of digging them, for use as a cemetery, with nothing to do with wooden posts. There are many other cremation burials in the bank and ditch at Stonehenge, so the theory is persuasive. On the other hand, it would seem unnecessary to create more or less regularly spaced holes simply for cremated bone, so the idea that the holes once supported posts still lingers.

In order to furnish proof that posts were once erected in the Aubrey Holes, the holes themselves ought to display flat bottoms and straight sides to show where posts had been, but they are rounded at the bottom and do not have straight sides. One suggestion is that originally there were posts in the holes, and cremations were buried around them, then the posts rotted away and the deposits and the soil slipped gradually down and filled the holes, obscuring the evidence for wooden posts. No one can be certain, but some reconstructions of the early version of Stonehenge show a ring of fifty-six wooden posts, and they may be correct.

Timber structures inside the circle

In the middle of the circle another array of post holes was discovered, one set indicating a fenced and possibly roofed passageway to or from the entrance in the south, leading to another set of holes in the centre of the monument, which are difficult if not impossible to interpret. One problem that besets the study of all the phases of Stonehenge is that excavations have concentrated on the eastern half of the circle, but despite the lack of knowledge about the western half, it is suggested that it is possible to discern concentric rings of post holes, similar to those found at Durrington Walls and the more ovoid rings of posts at Woodhenge, though these particular phases of these monuments belong to a later time than the very first phases of Stonehenge.

The structure may have been set up as a series of free-standing posts, and is sometimes represented as such in reconstruction drawings. No central post that could have supported a roof has been found belonging to this circular timber phase at Stonehenge, but it is still possible to interpret the wooden construction as a circular roofed building, with a large hole in the centre of the roof. The construction of such a roofed building would not have been beyond the capabilities of Neolithic carpenters. The whole set-up, roofed or not, has been dubbed as a cult centre, though the ceremonies that took place there are unknown and unknowable.

Problems of dating and chronology

The most important question about all these features of the first Stonehenge is whether they were all contemporary or successive, following each other in however many combinations that can be imagined. Were the banks and the ditch created to enclose a timber structure in the centre, or were the post holes inserted into the enclosure some time after it was built? Were the six rows of posts at the north-east entrance already there before the enclosure, dictating where the entrance should face, or were they set there at the same time that the ditch was dug, as an integral part of the entranceway, either to observe the moon or to provide a thicket of posts to act as a fence? Since the ditch surrounding the first Stonehenge seems to cut the post holes, it may be that the posts had already gone out of use before the circular enclosure was made, and may have been removed. Perhaps the cycles of the moon had been observed for long enough to be certain where the most northerly rising would occur and there was now another way of recording it without the rows of stakes. Another question, not yet resolved, is whether there were two standing stones located outside the entrance, namely the Heel Stone and its partner, before the circle was created, and were they used to mark the midsummer sunrise, dictating where the centre of the circle and its north-east entrance should lie?

At the south entrance it might seem that the passageway of wooden posts leading to the centre was related to the gap in the ditch and bank, which in turn may indicate that the enclosing circle came first and the timber structure was built inside it. As for the Aubrey Holes, the collective dating evidence from the finds suggests a date of 2800BC, which is later than the accepted date for the enclosing bank and ditch. However, this dating process dates the finds not the holes. Since the holes are laid out in a true circle, most likely by planting a stake in the centre and attaching a rope to swing round the entire circuit to mark the positions of the holes, it would seem that they predate the timber structure in the centre because anything that was erected in the middle of the bank and ditch would impede the marking out of a circle using this method, and it is difficult to understand how such a near-perfect circle could have been achieved in any other way. So either the Aubrey Holes were dug before the timber structure was built, or the timber structure came first but had been removed before the Aubrey Holes were made. Such speculation could go on *ad infinitum* and would prove nothing. The only possible answer is that all the features were definitely there, but possibly not all at the same time. Nobody knows the sequence of any of the component parts of the first Stonehenge, and more importantly nobody knows why they were built and what they were used for. Hopefully it may not always be so starkly negative.

4

THE NEOLITHIC BUILDERS OF STONEHENGE, *c.* 3100 BC TO *c.* 2400 BC

The Neolithic era comprises a very long time span from *c.* 4500 BC to *c.* 2400 BC. The beginning of the era marks the change from Mesolithic hunter-gatherer societies to farming, and the end of the era is discernible when the first metal tools and weapons start to appear, in the period now labelled as the Bronze Age, which began in the middle of the third millennium BC. Neither of these transitions, from Mesolithic to Neolithic, and from Neolithic to Bronze Age, was as abrupt as these bald statements make it sound.

Modern studies suggest that the full effects of what was once called the Neolithic Revolution, when farming was introduced, were very slow in coming to fruition, but this does not mean that there was complete stasis for centuries. To describe the people of the Neolithic era as though they were all the same, at all times and in all areas, remaining static for more than two thousand years, is patently absurd. Such a vast timescale, which in modern terms would extend from the current era as far back as the Iron Age, witnessed multiple changes that cannot be lumped together under a few headings. In the Neolithic era, the rate of change was probably much slower, but there would have been several shifts in customs and traditions, too slight to be easily detected and interpreted by archaeologists, who are allowed glimpses here and there at a limited number of sites, belonging to different timescales. In dealing simultaneously with the early and late Neolithic from its origins to its demise, with only sporadic evidence, anachronisms inevitably occur, compounded by a lack of precise dating evidence which could elucidate which aspects of Neolithic life were contemporary and which features predated or post-dated them.

It used to be thought that the Neolithic people must have been invaders. The disappearance of the Mesolithic hunter-gatherers was construed as the result of wholesale conquest and slaughter, but nowadays it is thought more likely that there was a blend of cultures, called 'acculturation' in archaeological terms, that saw the gradual reduction of hunting and gathering and the establishment of stock raising and agriculture. There is accumulating evidence that Mesolithic sites were still used in Neolithic times, and though such continuity of activity on the same sites does not entirely dispel the invasion and conquest theory, it is more likely that the Mesolithic hunter-gatherers were not eradicated. They simply became Neolithic farmers.

The process was probably very gradual. The Mesolithic way of life had served the population well enough for countless generations of people who knew how to keep warm and dry, and how to find shelters and food. This is not to say that a hunting and gathering lifestyle was entirely blissful and stress-free. A television programme some years ago followed the activities of a lady Flying Doctor working in Africa, ministering to the hunter-gatherer tribesmen and women of remote societies. The most common ailment that she was called upon to treat was stress and anxiety, mostly concerning worry about where the next meal was coming from.

Farming and the domestication of animals

If the development of farming was not the result of large-scale invasion, then it represents an influx of ideas, perhaps accompanied by groups of settlers but not conquering hordes who killed or drove the original population away. The spread of ideas still involves movement and communication on the part of some people, whether a small number of individuals, or of whole groups. New fashions in farming, pottery manufacture, and monument building may have been brought in by new people, or brought back from expeditions by native people who saw these things and liked them, or both. It is known that people did travel, since wooden trackways were built across marshy land, such as the Sweet Track, named after Raymond Sweet, who discovered it in the Somerset Levels. Roadways such as this would not have been constructed if nobody was going anywhere. There is ample evidence that people travelled for long distances, as revealed by the wide distribution of stones axes from the Lake District and from Wales, which are found many miles from their origin. Axes made of jadeite were also brought in from the Alpine regions and from France, at a time when Britain had long since been divorced from the Continental landmass by rising sea levels. These axes are usually formed by grinding the stone until it is smooth and highly polished, a process that would have taken many hours of patient labour. Some of them were work tools, but others, and especially the splendid jadeite axes from the Alps, were never used for anything as mundane as chopping down trees. They are interpreted as prestigious gifts, though from whom and to whom cannot be known. The important point is that some people knew the routes through Britain, and others knew how to cross the sea between Britain and the Continent, and thought it worthwhile to do so.

It is fairly certain now that the first domesticated animals represent imports from the Continent, rather than attempts to tame the local beasts in Britain. No one in their right mind would have attempted to domesticate the large wild cattle, the aurochs, which were not only enormous but would never have been described as gentle giants. They did not die out in Europe until relatively recent times, and their skeletons show how much larger they were than any of the domestic cattle whose bones have been found on Neolithic sites. On the other hand, the sheep and pigs native to Mesolithic Britain were smaller than the domesticated types whose bones are found on Neolithic sites, and it is thought that these larger animals could not have been the product of years of selective breeding.

It is possible that domestication of animals preceded agriculture. Domesticated animals would yield skins, fleeces, milk and meat. An analysis of cattle bones from a later Neolithic site revealed that many of the animals were older females, which strongly suggests that they were kept for breeding and milking before they were slaughtered. The presence of domesticated farm animals on early Neolithic archaeological sites need not always represent sedentary farmers who also grew crops. Animals can be herded and moved to new grazing areas, not necessarily migrating over long distances from summer to winter pastures, but simply moving on to better grasslands. Homes would therefore be transitory affairs, occupied for only a few seasons. It is possible that some sort of animal management had already started in Mesolithic times. In the southern Pennines archaeologists have suggested that the Mesolithic population controlled the herds of red deer, managing them so that they provided food and skins but without actually fully domesticating them, much as the Laplanders follow the reindeer herds and utilise them for food and leather, and as traction animals, but do not settle down to farm them in the same way that modern sheep or cattle farms are run. Remains of a domesticated dog were found at the Mesolithic site of Star Carr in Yorkshire. As Francis Pryor suggests, the herding instinct of dogs may have been exploited to round up prey animals. The idea of penning a few animals near to a temporary settlement site was perhaps not entirely revolutionary when the Neolithic people began to domesticate cattle, sheep and pigs.

When agriculture and crop growing was established, probably around 4500 to 4000 BC, hunting and gathering probably continued for some time, to supplement the food grown on the farms. The remains of wild animals found on Neolithic sites, such as hare and deer and other species, suggest that these were hunted to supplement the diet, and gathering wild food probably never died out. It seems that Neolithic people were fond of hazelnuts, raspberries and blackberries, for which there is archaeological evidence from some Neolithic sites.

Neolithic farmers used a simple plough called an ard, made of wood with a sharpened point, possibly fire hardened. This was drawn through the earth to create a fine soil for planting. The plough could have been pulled by oxen. As yet no ard plough has been found in Britain, but examples are known from Europe, and it is assumed that the same tool was used by British Neolithic people. The ard had no mould board to turn the soil over, so ploughing solely in one direction would only make small furrows in the earth and would not break up the soil very efficiently. Plough marks found on archaeological sites reveal that the farmers ploughed in criss-cross fashion, up and down the field in one direction, and then ploughing more or less at right angles across the original furrows, in order to ensure that the earth was fine enough for planting. There were regional variations in the quality of the soil, but most farmers were able to grow wheat and barley, as revealed by archaeological remains which turn up on various sites, and some early pottery was decorated by pressing grains into the clay.

When crops are to be grown, the people, or at least some of them, must remain in the same place to plant and nurture the crops, from the spring right through to the autumn. This presupposes that houses were built, storage facilities created, boundaries established and fences made to protect the crops from animals and birds, and possibly to guard against predatory neighbours – everything in fact that the territorial imperative demands.

Settlements and housing

Very little is known of Neolithic settlements in Britain, especially in the immediate area of Stonehenge. Just north of the monument itself, traces of a palisade have been found, stretching for 4,265 feet (1,300 metres), but it is not known if it was a demarcation boundary, or part of a large enclosure. Underneath some barrows, or burial mounds, traces of fences have been discovered, and it is suggested that the burial mounds were placed on the boundaries of the territories of family groups, for two reasons, one to make it clear whose land it was, and secondly to leave most of it free for crops and domesticated animals. Such demarcation of territory would have been perfectly possible for most if not all of the Neolithic farms, but the marking of boundaries or individual fields must remain hypothetical, supported by some few pieces of evidence on the ground. Fences leave little trace for archaeologists, who would be readily able to recognise them but incredibly lucky to find them, and even luckier to be able to trace a complete fence all the way round a Neolithic settlement or an individual field.

Evidence for Neolithic houses is problematical. Post holes have been found representing rectangular buildings, but the use to which the buildings were put is debated. What were once confidently labelled as dwellings have been reinterpreted by some archaeologists as mortuary houses for the dead, not dwelling places for the living. The presence of hearths inside these structures, which ought to confirm the sites as dwellings, are just as problematical, since they are mostly later insertions. As ever, more research is needed.

In the area immediately around Stonehenge there are a few signs of settlements, but these are represented by scatters of flints and some pottery, with no sign of houses or any buildings that can be interpreted as farms. More positive evidence for houses has been found north of Stonehenge, at Durrington Walls, where rectangular platforms, interpreted as house floors, have been found outside the bank and ditch enclosure. These are situated to the north of the passageway, or Avenue, leading from the south-east entrance to the River Avon. Similar examples of house floors have been identified close to Woodhenge, but although these so-called houses were probably contemporary with the later phases of Stonehenge, they were established later than the first version of the bank and ditch enclosure.

The most limiting factor which makes it difficult to identify Neolithic houses is that they would not be permanent structures used by successive generations of kin-groups. Even in medieval times, houses were less substantial or permanent than modern ones. Excavations at the deserted medieval village of Wharram

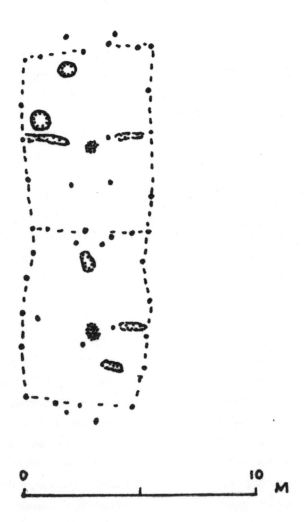

0   10 M

Fig. 7. The first Stonehenge people left a truly magnificent monument but few traces of how they lived. Neolithic dwellings are notoriously difficult to find, because houses would not be in permanent long-term occupation, and being built of wood their remains would not survive. This plan shows a structure that has been interpreted as a Neolithic house near Buxton, Derbyshire. There was more than one such building on this site but they are not generally thought to be contemporary, and cannot be interpreted as the remains of a village. The so-called houses were probably successive, as one house decayed and a new one was built. No house site so far discovered displays any trace of running repairs, suggesting that people abandoned old houses and moved on. At the henge at Durrington Walls, where it is thought that the Stonehenge people lived, house floors have been identified. Drawn by Jacqui Taylor after Pryor 2004.

Percy in Yorkshire revealed that houses were regularly pulled down and rebuilt, approximately every two decades or so, though the village remained in occupation until its final abandonment. Neolithic houses would be less long-lived and would not be grouped in villages. Three so-called houses at Buxton are thought to be successive, not contemporary. Everything points to movement of Neolithic settlement sites on a regular basis. No evidence has yet been found for the renovation of existing buildings, nor is there any evidence that houses were torn down and rebuilt in situ like the medieval ones at Wharram Percy. The current theory is that people moved on when the soil was exhausted, but perhaps not very far away, not constituting a migration to more fertile lands.

Pottery and tools

The best indicators of settlement are pottery, tools and weapons. Pottery studies have revealed a wide variety of types, usually named after the site or sites where remains have been found. There are many types and styles of Neolithic pottery, intensively studied and categorised. To oversimplify somewhat, there are two main styles of pottery found on and around Neolithic sites, one known as Peterborough Ware, named after the place where examples were first discovered, and Grooved Ware, named after the physical appearance of the vessels. Peterborough Ware consists of round-bottomed vessels, the bodies of which were marked by pressing objects into the clay, such as ears of corn or twisted ropes. This ware is chiefly, but not exclusively, associated with burials and death. Grooved Ware is flat-bottomed, and marked (unsurprisingly) by grooves along the surface of the clay. It is more practical, and associated with living people. These hypothetical rules do not

Fig. 8. Some examples of Neolithic pottery labelled Grooved Ware from its decoration. This pottery was used extensively throughout Britain and Ireland, but is not known on the Continent. The pots were hand-made by building up coiled layers of clay to form the vessels, since wheel-thrown pottery was not to be introduced until the distant future. Drawn by Jacqui Taylor after Pollard 2002.

apply to all archaeological sites. The two styles of pottery are not exactly contemporary, and contrary to the theory that they were associated with life and death, Grooved Ware occasionally appears with burials and Peterborough Ware turns up in settlement contexts. The distribution of Grooved Ware was widespread, as revealed by its former name, Rinyo-Clacton Ware, bestowed on this style of pottery when it became clear from excavations that it was used all over Britain from Rinyo in the Orkneys to Clacton in Essex. Although Grooved Ware permeated throughout Britain and Ireland, no examples of Grooved Ware have been found on the Continent. Nor does it turn up except on rare occasions at Stonehenge, which may reinforce the interpretation of Stonehenge as a place of death, and Grooved Ware as the preferred vessels for the living.

Neolithic pots were made by building up successive layers of clay, tempered by mixing the clay with gravel or other substances, which prevented cracking during the firing process. Wheel-thrown pottery belongs to the very distant future. It is unlikely that there was a factory system and a distribution mechanism for these pots, so it may have been local families who made the pots at home, and it was simply the techniques and the fashions which spread rather than the pots themselves. Local families made their own pots, which would account for the great variety of designs and patterns, and for the sometimes poor quality of the vessels.

Specialised tools were already in use in Mesolithic times, when people were expert at shaping flints, and they utilised wood and bone for a variety of purposes. Flint was used for the manufacture of cutting edges such as knives and axes, and for scrapers, arrowheads and harpoons. Neolithic people continued to use flint for tools and also began to make stone axes. The sites where the stone was obtained for these axes, for example Great Langdale in Cumbria, were often remote and inaccessible, implying that the type of stone was very important, perhaps more for ritual purposes than for daily use. Suitable stones were available in less remote areas, but were not exploited. Apart from their use as symbolic and prestige goods, stone axes enabled Neolithic farmers to cut down trees and clear land on a larger scale than their predecessors.

Other tools were made of bone and wood. Antler picks found on many sites show how ditches were dug, and animal shoulder blades were used as shovels. Bone was used for toggles and dress ornament, and wood for handles of knives and axes. Bone and wood were used to make a variety of pins. Carpentry techniques were well advanced in Neolithic times, as indicated by the Sweet Track, consisting of hurdles laid across the ground, well founded and

pinned down with wooden pegs. The Neolithic people understood
the best uses of different kinds of wood, and may have managed
woodlands, using pollarding and coppicing to provide them with
stakes, rods and pegs. These woodworkers were perfectly capable
of building houses with timber frames utilising a variety of joints,
probably using basket-weave infill sections daubed with clay just
as medieval builders used wattle and daub.

For weapons, Neolithic people used flint for their arrowheads.
Their bows, examples of which have been found preserved in the
timber trackways in the Somerset Levels, were comparable in
size with the medieval longbow, and perhaps almost as powerful.
Hunting game was clearly not the only purpose of the bows and
arrows, as demonstrated by a burial near Peterborough where the
remains of a man, a woman and two children were found. The
man had an arrow still in his body when he was interred. These
are not the only remains which show evidence of violent death. A
disturbing number of skulls show signs of fatal head wounds. The
accumulation of evidence now enables archaeologists to speak of
Neolithic warfare, rather than just a series of domestic murders or
ritual sacrifices. This in turn presupposes some level of organisation,
the existence of warrior chiefs or leaders, involving territorial
disputes, or at least an ultimate corporate goal to be achieved on
the part of the aggressors, and lives and property worth defending
on the part of the people who were under attack.

Neolithic society

The structure of Neolithic society cannot be illustrated. More is
known about what happened to the dead than about how people
lived, but analysis of skeletal remains reveals that many people
suffered from arthritis, especially in the lower back, and several

people had abscesses on their teeth. Neolithic life was not very comfortable.

For the early Neolithic era, the burial chambers of the long barrows contain remains of relatively few individuals, and the small numbers cannot be representative of the whole population. It is tempting to interpret the remains in the barrows as those of the elite class or of the leaders of society, but there is no way of proving this hypothesis. It is not possible to speak of tribes and leaders, but at the same time the building of the communal earthworks such as the barrows, causewayed enclosures and cursus monuments, all requiring thousands of man-hours to construct, strongly implies that there was a person or a group of people who originated and managed the proceedings, and persuaded many others to assist in the building works. The decision to close the burial chambers and bury them inside a long barrow had to begin with a person or a family group. The decision to build a causewayed enclosure or a cursus may have started in the same way but these massive projects could never have been carried out by a small family group. Someone in charge of the building operations is lurking unknown and unknowable to modern archaeologists and historians.

It is suggested that the individual straight sections of ditches at all Neolithic monuments were allocated to family groups, but there is no information as to what 'family group' means in practical terms. If life expectancy was only thirty or forty years, as suggested by archaeologists, then this precludes the idea of families of several generations. Even if people started to produce children in their early teens they would not live long enough to see many grandchildren, let alone great-grandchildren. A cult of the ancestors may have substituted for the lack of living examples within the family. Though it is clear that elaborate rituals were performed for the dead, it is not clear whether people were remembered individually. When the bones of the dead were placed all together in such jumbled fashion in many barrows, it is difficult to see how the remains could be associated with specific individuals, so the dead were probably remembered, revered and propitiated as spirits. Did Neolithic people subscribe to the concept of extended families, with uncles and aunts and cousins? Did they undergo marriage ceremonies, performed within the causewayed enclosures, as is taken for granted in most accounts of Neolithic life? Were they monogamous, or were women held in common and the children brought up by all members of the group? Or was society originally matriarchal? In pastoral societies, male dominance is usually taken as read, and the Neolithic farmers, with their presumed transitory settlements and emphasis on stock raising, were probably no different. Anything is possible and nothing is known.

If Neolithic society was not organised in village groups and if life was very short, there was probably a need for some communal focal point. In modern villages there are (or were) several focal points serving a variety of purposes – the village hall, the pub, the church, the school – where different groups could meet for different social, educational and religious functions. It is possible that the so-called causewayed enclosures fulfilled similar multiple purposes for early Neolithic groups. From the finds in these enclosures it is clear that people met there, possibly for extended periods, but the absence of houses or any evidence of longer-term settlement suggests that people did not live there permanently. The causewayed enclosures were probably used for ceremonials and festivals, perhaps even for some rudimentary governmental functions, perhaps with authority figures standing in judgement over disputes. Some gatherings may have been conducted along the lines of, 'We are called here today because we are going to fell several trees and make posts to create a wooden circle with a bank and ditch round it. Bring your axes, your antler picks, your shoulder-blade shovels and your wicker baskets, and don't forget food supplies for several days.' The unavoidable conclusion for modern people is that there was someone in charge of what went on in causewayed enclosures. There may have been a priestly caste to oversee religious ceremonies, conduct the rites of the dead, and perhaps to watch the skies for the well-being of the community. There may have been leaders who directed communal activities. In some societies these two roles, of priest and leader, are combined in the same person or group.

The emergence of some sort of leader or leaders is implied by the theory that Neolithic people engaged in warfare, as mentioned above. Gang fighting can erupt spontaneously, but when fighting is labelled as warfare someone has to organise it and give orders to the participants. A warrior society may have grown up, possibly demonstrated by an analysis of cremated remains from Stonehenge. After early twentieth-century excavations at the monument, a collection of the cremated bones were all gathered together and buried in Aubrey Hole number 7, with a plaque explaining their presence in this single hole. In those days there was little interest in the bones because there were no techniques available for extracting information from them, but at least the remains were not thrown away, and it was fortunate that records were kept about what had happened to them. These remains were recently dug up in excavations conducted by Mike Parker Pearson, and on analysis it was revealed that the bones belonged to about fifty individuals. These were predominantly the bones of healthy, robust men between twenty to forty years old. It is speculated that they were the leaders of society who may have originated and conducted the building of Stonehenge, but they may also have been warriors specially selected, perhaps because of their prowess in safeguarding the community or waging war against perceived enemies. Their cremation and burial at Stonehenge may have been carried out in order to reward and honour them after death.

Leadership or even royalty may be illustrated by the demise of communal burials in long barrows and the rise of individual burials, or cremations, of single corpses. This change had already begun as far back as 3500 BC, and indicates that there was a new ideology in Neolithic society, overlapping for a long time with the old ways. Cremations became more fashionable than burials. Perhaps the burials represent certain highly regarded or powerful individuals, especially if grave goods are buried with the person, but the inclusion of grave goods for the dead does not seem to have occurred until much later Neolithic times or in the very early Bronze Age. Cremations perhaps became more common because it was a much quicker method of releasing the spirit than de-fleshing a corpse and then sorting and burying the bones.

How far did the knowledge and use of Stonehenge spread in Britain in Neolithic times? What made so many people come to Stonehenge and bury the cremated remains of their dead in the earthen bank and in the Aubrey Holes? It is speculated that they came from a large catchment area to do so, which suggests that the monument was a very important cemetery full of religious meaning to contemporary people, incorporating beliefs probably stretching back to Mesolithic times. Was there someone in charge of the bank and ditch complex, or even the whole of the surrounding area, who gave permission for burials? There may have been some sort of communal ceremonial attached to each visit, or it may simply be that families came and did the honours without ceremony. Did they hold feasts, chant or sing, and perform their dances? Were there priest/shamans who conducted all types of ceremonies, for the dead, and for the observance of the phases of the moon and the rising and setting of the sun at midsummer and midwinter? Did they use hallucinogenic drugs, as evidenced by the remains of such substances found in a pot from Scotland? The plethora of question marks indicates that the answers are not known for certain. They can perhaps be provided by studying the practices of tribal peoples from modern times, such as the Native Americans and the tribes of Africa, Australia, South America and New Guinea. Ultimately, frustrating though it is, no one can know all aspects of the mindset of late Neolithic people in Britain.

The abandonment of Stonehenge

In the later Neolithic period, in the middle of the third millennium, there was a change for the worse in society, and settlement patterns probably changed. Some of the causewayed enclosures were fortified, such as Crickley Hill in Gloucestershire, where the surrounding ditches and causeways giving access to the site were replaced by a much deeper ditch, with no causeways and only two entrances. More permanent settlement is detected inside the enclosure, with houses aligned along what can be interpreted as streets. Areas seem to have been assigned to specific purposes, such as flint working, and some areas were set aside for rituals. At this former causewayed enclosure, archaeologists discovered hundreds of arrowheads, all accumulated around the entrances and ramparts, indicating that ferocious attacks had taken place there. At a similar causewayed enclosure site at Hambledon Hill in Dorset, there is evidence of violent attacks, bodies being thrown into the ditch and left there instead of being respectfully buried. The fate of these two former causewayed enclosures, and the fortifications that were constructed at other causewayed enclosures, may not be representative of events all over the country, but it seems that at around the same time, areas that had formerly been cleared of woodland had become overgrown and regeneration of tree cover had begun, suggesting a decline in the farming population, probably caused by endemic violence, possibly food shortages, or some disaster as yet undetected. One theory is that far distant volcanic eruptions in other parts of the world could have caused changes in the weather, which in turn would entail crop failures, near starvation, and probably warfare among surviving rival groups.

Probably at about this time, around the mid-third millennium BC, people stopped coming to Stonehenge. The site became overgrown and neglected, no one dug out and cleaned the ditch any longer, and trees grew in the banks. The first phase of Stonehenge was ended.

5

THE FIRST STONES
OF STONEHENGE,
c. 2550 BC TO *c.* 2450 BC

In the 1950s archaeological excavations revealed a series of paired holes in the eastern half of the ditch and bank enclosure. Sockets where stones had once stood were clearly discerned, but, just as clearly, whatever had stood in these holes had been removed and the holes had been obliterated in prehistoric times, when the later versions of Stonehenge were built. The holes as excavated form a semi-circle, and are labelled Q and R holes, the Q holes being the outer row and the R holes the inner row. The R holes run in a slightly more closely spaced circle than the Q holes, as if each set of two holes had been laid out like the spokes of a wheel radiating from the centre. The shapes of the excavated holes look like dumb-bells and are sometimes referred to as such.

The Q and R holes raise many questions. They form an arc on the eastern side, but since the western half of the interior of Stonehenge has not been excavated, it is impossible to ascertain whether or not holes were dug on this side to form a complete circle. Three main theories have been proposed by archaeologists, none of them as yet capable of proof. There may have been a double circle of stones, possibly with an entrance to the north-east like the earlier bank and ditch. An alternative theory is that it was originally intended to create a complete circle, but for reasons unknown it was never finished. Other scholars are quite certain that the prehistoric builders planned and built only the semi-circle, sometimes called a horseshoe, but reconstruction plans and drawings of the supposed semi-circle vary a little as to precisely where the open half of it was situated.

Some of the holes contained fragments of Bluestones, and because there are several Bluestones within the final version of Stonehenge, it is suggested that the Q and R holes once held upright Bluestones which were removed when the Sarsen Stones were erected, and after a long interval were reused. It can never be proven that all the Q and R holes held the same kind of stone, but if there was a complete double circle of Bluestones, there would probably have been about eighty of them. The date when this stone circle or semi-circle was set up is now thought to have been about 2550 BC, revising the earlier theories which placed it much later, in about 2100 BC. This new project was started after Stonehenge had been abandoned for some time and had become quite overgrown. The duration of the abandonment is not fully established, perhaps starting from about 2900 BC and continuing until the middle of the third millennium, a period of about 500 years when many generations of people perhaps ignored the area. It is possible that there was some continued use of the site for cremation burials even though trees and weeds had more or less taken over, but this cannot be proven. Then, after a lapse of some centuries, for some unfathomable reason the prehistoric people of the area reclaimed and renovated Stonehenge.

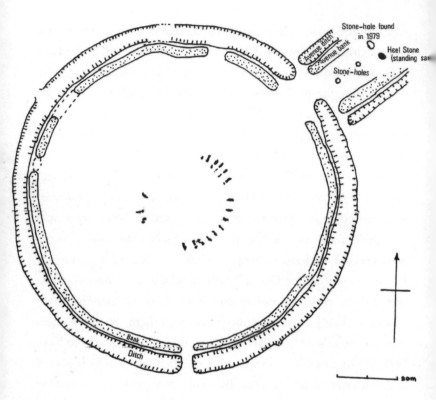

Fig. 9. The first stone circle at Stonehenge replaced an earlier wooden structure or structures. Post holes were found in the twentieth-century excavations leading from the entrance in the south to a possible roofed building supported by circles of posts in the centre of the bank and ditch enclosure. This was removed and about 2550 BC pairs of stones were set up in two concentric circles. The evidence for this was found during excavation of the eastern sector of the monument, which revealed a series of paired holes, described as dumb-bell from their plans. These were labelled Q and R holes. They contained fragments of Bluestones, and so the whole feature was interpreted as a Double Bluestone Circle, though not everyone agrees that the circuit was ever completed. The western sector has not been excavated, so there is no proof for a complete circle or the absence of it. The Bluestone controversy splits archaeologists and geologists into two camps. The geological origin of the stones is the Preseli mountains in south-west Wales, but it is disputed whether the stones arrived at Stonehenge via human agency or whether geological action carried the stones to somewhere within the vicinity of the monument that was built with them. For geologists, who agree on the origin of the stones, the major dispute concerns the distance and direction that glaciers travelled. The Avenue shown on this plan may have been contemporary with this phase of Stonehenge, but some scholars prefer to date it to a later period, contemporary with the Sarsen Circle. Drawn by Jacqui Taylor after Darvill 2007.

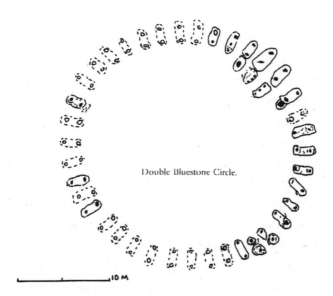

Fig. 10. A more detailed plan of the Double Bluestone Circle. Solid lines represent the Q and R holes that were revealed by excavation, dotted lines represent the conjectural holes, based on the premise that the circle was complete and calculated according to the spacing of the holes in the eastern sector. Drawn by Jacqui Taylor after Darvill 2007.

The problem with the Bluestones

There is less controversy about the date of this early stone version of Stonehenge than there is about where the stones came from. Geologically, there is no problem. The stones derive from outcrops in the Preseli hills in south-west Wales, where oblong slabs jut out of the rock formation looking as though they could be picked off with ease. The rocks in this region were formed as part of the Fishguard Volcanic Group, where eruptions extended as far as the Preseli area. The Bluestones at Stonehenge are not all the same kind of stone, some being dolerite, others rhyolite. Both are igneous rocks, but dolerite is more like basalt, with coarse grains, whereas rhyolite has finer grains, being often formed from volcanic ash flowing in gas clouds of very high temperature. All the

Bluestones share a common characteristic, that when broken they are blue or green inside.

The major problem which has not yet been conclusively solved concerns how some of these stones arrived at Stonehenge. There are two opposed theories, one adhering to the possibility that stones were brought to the site by teams of Neolithic people, and the other claiming that the stones were already lying somewhere near Stonehenge, having been moved there by glaciers many centuries before Stonehenge was even thought of. Geological and chemical analyses of the Stonehenge Bluestones over the past years have failed to settle the dispute. Two different investigations have produced completely different conclusions. One series of tests revealed that the Bluestones of Stonehenge do not come from one particular restricted location in the Preseli hills, but from a variety of different sites within the range of hills, which makes it more likely that they were brought to the vicinity of Stonehenge by the random distribution of glacial action. More recently, another series of tests conflicts with this conclusion. Fragments of Bluestones from Stonehenge were examined and analysed, the results pinpointing the origin of the stones at one particular specific site in the Preseli hills, at Craig Rhos-y-Felin. This conclusion is cited in support of the theory that Neolithic people went to Wales and chose their stones from one location. The debate is not yet conclusively ended because four standing Bluestones at Stonehenge do not match the petrographical analysis of the majority of the fragments that have been analysed. Back to the drawing board?

It used to be accepted almost unconditionally that the prehistoric people of Wiltshire went on an expedition to south-west Wales to extract the Bluestones and conveyed them all back overland and across water to the site of Stonehenge. This theory was strengthened by a passage from the work of Geoffrey of Monmouth, who lived *c.* 1100 to 1156 and wrote his *Historia Regum Britanniae (History of the Kings of Britain)* around 1136. His narrative is not generally credited with accuracy, to say the least, but when he refers to Merlin bringing the stones for Stonehenge from a place called Killaraus in Ireland, it has been suggested that there was a very ancient tradition that the stones had come from somewhere in the west. This implies that the oral tradition had survived in Britain through the Bronze Age, the Iron Age, the Roman period and the Norman invasion. All things are possible of course, so perhaps some tales really were carried from generation to generation. Sadly Geoffrey provided no details as to how Merlin might have moved the stones. He 'floated' them, but this does not necessarily mean that he put them on boats. Merlin was after all a magician and could make the stones fly if he wished. Geoffrey did not refer to Wales as the origin of the stones, and more importantly he was not necessarily referring to the Bluestones. In his day the overwhelming vision of Stonehenge would have been of very large Sarsen Stones, some of them capped with lintels, while the Bluestones, though arranged within the circle, are much smaller and less notable, and most importantly they do not have lintels. A medieval illustration of Geoffrey's book, painted long after he first wrote it, shows Merlin casually placing one of the lintels on top of two uprights, while watched by two suitably awestruck companions. Despite these caveats, the work of Geoffrey of Monmouth has become almost inextricably related to the Bluestones and their transport from the west.

Various modern experiments have been tried out to transport heavy stones over a short distance, not all the way from Wales to Wiltshire, in order to test the theories about how they were moved.

It is suggested that prehistoric people used sledges, either directly in contact with the ground surface, or mounted on rollers, which could be lubricated with animal fat. This implies a lot of dead animals and a veritable orgy of feasting. One of the greatest problems in using sledges on wooden rollers or by themselves is that the ground has to be firm and flat, so almost insuperable problems are presented by an uneven landscape, marshy areas, and hills. Heavy weights on rollers are almost impossible to transport without laying trackways first. This is not beyond the capabilities of Neolithic people, but there is as yet no evidence for such trackways for the Bluestones, certainly not all the way from Wales. Even with prepared tracks, the use of sledges on rollers is not straightforward. If the rollers are not uniform in length and also in circumference they clog up together, rather than rolling smoothly underneath the sledge. There is also the danger that the sledge will slew around and fall off the rollers. This is not to deny the possibility of transporting the stones on sledges mounted on top of a wooden base, but this base is much more manageable if the wood is made into large planks, similar to railway sleepers. From a later time and another part of the world, a bas relief from Kujundschik shows how the Assyrians transported a huge statue of a man-headed bull on a sledge, using flat pieces of wood that are clearly shown underneath the sledge, and planks are scattered all around as several men gather them up and replace them at the front of the sledge. At the rear men are shown with huge levers holding the sledge steady and easing its passage onto the sleepers. Friction between the base of the sledge and its wooden planks may have been reduced by oil or water. Progress would have been slow, distances were probably quite short, and level ground would have been desirable, but this method would be more stable than using rollers.

If the stones were conveyed from Wales, it is suggested that they must have been ferried across the Severn estuary and unloaded on its southern shore. For water transport it is envisaged that the stones were loaded onto dug-out canoes roped together, or perhaps some other small boats would be used. People were already crossing the Channel between the Continent and Britain, so shipping was probably quite advanced. However, although the transport of heavy stones may be feasible once the boat or boats are loaded, it is extremely difficult to place the stones onto boats without slippage, especially from a riverbank with no helpful quayside structures and lifting gear to assist in the process.

Of course, it is important not to underestimate what late Neolithic or early Bronze Age people could achieve. Stonehenge itself bears witness to tremendous lifting power and technical skill. But unfortunately no modern experiment has yet succeeded in showing how prehistoric transport of the Bluestones for about 150 miles (225 kilometres), most of the route on land and some of it across water, may have been carried out. This does not mean that the experiments were totally useless, because they all served to show just how hard it was to move the stones, and how far away from the prehistoric mindset we moderns are. One day someone may hit on the answer, but up to now, in modern reconstructions, stones have been dragged for only a few miles using manpower; and more importantly, people-power was sometimes assisted by modern lifting machinery. In modern experiments conducted so far, no stone has yet been conveyed across water on canoes or skin boats without being tipped overboard and lost.

Nevertheless, the Bluestones were obviously moved from somewhere to Stonehenge, by prehistoric people possibly using sledges on rollers or whatever method they devised. The question is how far did they have to move the stones? This is where archaeologists and geologists do battle. In one corner there are those who favour long-distance transport by humans from Wales, and in the other corner there are geologists and some archaeologists who favour the theory that it was the action of glaciers that brought the Bluestones to the Salisbury Plain, hundreds of thousands of years before Stonehenge was built.

A controversial Bluestone found in a barrow near to Stonehenge complicates matters even further. It had been used to seal the entrance to Boles Barrow, which was excavated by William Cunnington in 1801. This stone has been claimed by the supporters of the geological glacial theory as proof that the Bluestones arrived well before Stonehenge was built, because the barrow predates the monument. But a counter-argument has been put forward, suggesting that the barrow was sealed up a very long time after it was built, and the Bluestone used for this purpose came from Stonehenge, specifically from the Bluestone Horseshoe inside the Trilithons. The theory goes that the Bluestone Horseshoe was once a completely enclosed oval, since holes have been found in the opening which may once have supported stones. According to this reasoning, the original oval was reshaped by the removal of the stones at the north-east end to produce the Horseshoe that is visible now. It has been suggested that when this occurred, one of these stones may have been taken from Stonehenge to the barrow and used to close the entrance.

The Bluestone that was once inside the barrow is in itself a mystery. Even its current whereabouts is disputed. A stone in the Salisbury and South Wiltshire Museum is said to be the Boles Barrow stone, brought there in 1934. Before that it was in

William Cunnington's garden along with other stones, and was removed from there to Heytesbury House, and then finally to the Museum. It was called the Stonehenge stone, but the evidence for this is based on tradition rather than an archaeological log denoting its different locations with drawings and latterly with photographs, accompanied by the dates each time it was moved. This lack of solid evidence allows for a small loophole for dissenters. There are some archaeologists who dispute the origin of this stone, claiming that the one in Salisbury Museum is not the Bluestone from Boles Barrow. Wherever the stone is now, and whatever its early location, without properly authenticated documentation on all its movements from the date when it was taken out of the earth in 1801 to its arrival at the Museum, it can only be said that it existed, and its mere existence does not provide unqualified proof that glacial movement brought it and other stones to a location near Stonehenge, long before the monument was built.

The greatest geological debate concerns how far south the glaciers of the successive Ice Ages travelled, and in which direction the ice flowed. On these points not even the geologists agree with each other. Since this is a short book about Stonehenge and not a geological textbook, it only remains to point out that glacial action may have brought the Bluestones within reach of Stonehenge, and they were collected and used by the local people who revived the monument after a long period of neglect. Transport would not have been easy, as modern experiments have shown, but if the stones were lying on the ground somewhere near Stonehenge where the glacier had deposited them, then obviously they would only have to be conveyed for a few miles overland instead of hundreds of miles across land and sea.

The numbers of stones that were brought to the site of Stonehenge is also debatable. If there was a complete double circle, over eighty Bluestones would have been required, but since there are only just over forty Bluestones at Stonehenge now, it may be that the half-circle was all that was ever planned and built. This in turn means that the effort involved in the haulage of the stones would be halved, not that this helps in finding out how it was done.

The reasons why the people of the mid-third millennium set up a circle or half-circle of Bluestones are even harder to establish. It is claimed that the Bluestones were perceived as magical, or as having healing properties. Some of the scholars who consider that the stones were brought from Wales by human agency suggest that they were specifically sought out because of these properties, and Stonehenge became a healing and religious centre, attracting devotees from far and wide. It has also been suggested that it was not the prehistoric people of the Stonehenge area who transported the stones, but the inhabitants of early Wales who brought them to the new centre. Another theory concerns the prehistoric people of Brittany, who have been credited with the building of the first stone circle, or half-circle, at Stonehenge. Cross-Channel links were established between Brittany and Britain, and horseshoe monuments are more common in Brittany, so it is a relatively short step to the development of the idea that the Bluestones were deliberately arranged by an influx of ancient Bretons, in a semi-circular horseshoe shape, which was never intended to be a complete circuit. It is quite possible that influence spread from Brittany, but an invasion of Bretons taking over the disused monument and reviving it by trekking to and from Wales with special stones is somewhat less likely.

The Station Stones

Another feature of Stonehenge which may have been established at about this time is the positioning of the four so-called Station Stones, sometimes referred to as the Four Stations Stones. These were placed at the corners of an almost perfect rectangle, framing the Bluestones. According to the numbering system for the components of Stonehenge, the Station Stones are labelled from 91 to 94, starting with Stone 91, situated on the east side, or to the right of the north-east entrance as seen from inside the monument. The other three stones are numbered in clockwise fashion. Stone 91 is the only complete one, but although it was more or less upright in the eighteenth century it had already started to lean over, and is now recumbent. Stone 93 is a rounded stump, a shadow of its former self, presumably once much taller. A bank and ditch was dug at some unknown date enclosing the vanished Stones 92 and 94, and because the earth structures looked like barrows, they were labelled as such by early investigators. Though there are no stones to be seen now, excavations revealed that stones had once stood there but had been removed. The Station Stones are Sarsens, not Bluestones. They were not shaped or smoothed, existing in their natural state like the Heel Stone, and in fact like the stones in other stone circles in the British Isles.

There are no lines of stones set between the four corners to mark out the long and short sides of the rectangle, and because only two stones were still visible, early antiquarians could not necessarily see the significance of the Station Stones, since the rectangle that they formed was obscured by the Sarsen Circle, and all that was visible was one leaning stone, one stump and two sets of small circular banks and ditches, appearing as mounds which were thought to mark the sites of burials. In the nineteenth century it was suggested that the mounds were the observation points for use in combination with the two remaining stones, since the midsummer sunrise could be seen by standing on the site of the vanished Stone 92 and looking towards Stone 91.

There is much debate about exactly which phase of Stonehenge these Four Station Stones belong to, so in some accounts they are said to be earlier than the first Bluestone Circle, and in other accounts they are said to belong to a later phase. As noted above, all that can be said is that they were later than the Aubrey Holes, and earlier than the circle of Sarsen Stones. The ditch around Stone 92 ran around three Aubrey Holes in the south, suggesting that the holes had gone out of use and had been filled in, so there would have been no sign of them when the Station Stones were set up and the two banks and ditches around Stones 92 and 94 were dug. The presence of the Sarsen Circle would have obscured the sight-lines along the diagonals of the rectangle, so it is almost certain that the Station Stones were established before the Sarsen ring. This speculative dating for the establishment of the Station Stones, after the Aubrey Holes and before the Sarsen Circle, still encompasses many years, centuries even, so it can hardly be said to be precise.

The purpose of the Station Stones may have been to make astronomical observations. The short sides of the rectangle are parallel to the alignment of Stonehenge itself, running north-east to south-west, and could be associated with the midsummer sunrise and the midwinter sunset. The lines of the long sides focus on the rising and setting of the moon. Another feature is that diagonal lines drawn from Stone 92 to 94, and from Stone 91 to 93, cross at the centre of Stonehenge, and so the four stones may have been used in this way to mark the centre for the erection of the Sarsen Circle.

6

STONEHENGE AS WE KNOW IT,
c. 2450 BC TO *c.* 1800 BC

The final phases of Stonehenge consist of the components that are visible today. The stone version of Stonehenge would have taken a very long time to build, and there were modifications as time went on, so it should be pointed out that the separate features that confront visitors nowadays were not all set in place at the same time. If we describe what can be seen without regard to chronology, moving from outside the stone monument to the centre, the first component of the stone circle is formed from thirty uprights and thirty lintels, though the absence of stones in the south-west sector has been used to support the theory that the circle was never actually completed. As already mentioned in the Introduction, when Sir Flinders Petrie surveyed and numbered the stones, numbers were allocated to the places where upright stones and lintels ought to be, judging from the dimensions of the remaining stones and their spacing. Some authors, favouring the idea of a completed circle with all thirty stones in place, have suggested that over the succeeding centuries the missing stones were taken away to be used for various purposes, but it is impossible to trace them and to be able to say where they all went, whole or in broken sections.

It may be true that the circle was never finished, or perhaps the monument was never even planned as a circle in the first place, but it is probably much more satisfying for modern visitors to conceive of a complete circle with lintels running round the top than it is to envisage a half or three-quarter circle open on one side, either originally designed that way or simply left unfinished.

A puzzling factor about the Sarsen Circle is the truncated height of Stone 11, which appears to have been inserted in its current state rather than erected as one of the uprights and then reduced in size. One suggestion is that a timber structure may have been built on top of the stone to compensate for its lack of elevation. This may be so, but the unanswerable question is why a full-size stone was not erected when the builders showed themselves to be perfectly capable of finding, shaping and raising all the other stones.

As we continue with the description of the monument from the outside to the inside, all round the inner face of the Sarsen Circle there are the smaller Bluestones, most likely dismantled from the original Double Bluestone Circle, or possibly only a half-circle, and perhaps stored somewhere nearby, and then brought back inside when the Sarsen Circle and the Horseshoe were built. Inside the circles of Sarsen Stones and Bluestones, there were five sets of Trilithons, arranged in a horseshoe formation, with the open end facing the entrance in the north-east. Some of the stones have fallen down, so the complete structure in its erstwhile glory is not visible now. Early reconstruction drawings from the sixteenth century onwards show not an open-ended horseshoe, but a completely enclosed oval, or even a circle, with Trilithons all around it. Given the looting of stones that occurred over the centuries this is not a total impossibility. The theory that the smaller Bluestone structure, lining the inside of the Trilithon Horseshoe, was once an enclosed oval has been mentioned above in connection with the Bluestone from the Boles Barrow. There are other horseshoe enclosures that have been found in Britain, and they are much more frequently found in Brittany. Finds on prehistoric sites have been used to demonstrate links across the Channel between Brittany and Britain, so the predilection on the Continent for horseshoe-shaped stone monuments may have influenced the builders of Stonehenge. As ever, the supposed influence from Brittany has been disputed, on the grounds that it is possible that horseshoe monuments developed spontaneously and separately in different areas. The Trilithon arrangement is what sets Stonehenge apart from the other horseshoes that are known at several sites in England and Wales as well as in Brittany. These horseshoes are usually built from single standing stones, not dressed and shaped stones like those of the Trilithons, and more importantly the other horseshoes do not possess lintels.

The openings of both the Trilithon and the Bluestone Horseshoes face the north-east entrance to Stonehenge, and from this arrangement it can be argued, albeit without undeniable proof, that there was never a complete oval enclosure. The purpose may have been to capture the midsummer sunrise as the light entered the monument through the arms of the Bluestone and Trilithon Horseshoes, penetrating to the curve at the rear. The modern perception of Stonehenge is indelibly focused on the midsummer sunrise, but it is equally possible that prehistoric observers may also have watched the midwinter sunset, which is visible for a few dramatic moments before it sinks down to the horizon. It cannot be accidental that in midwinter the setting sun is framed in a rectangular viewing box, the vertical sides of which are formed by the two largest Trilithons, Stones 55 and 56, and the horizontal sides by the Trilithon lintel 156 and the lower lintel of the Sarsen Circle. It is comparable to the roof box at the tomb at Newgrange. At Stonehenge and elsewhere, there may have been religious ceremonies in midwinter. It was probably considered vital to perform such ceremonies, perhaps accompanied by chanting, singing and dancing, possibly even sacrifice, to ensure that the sun halted its progression along the horizon, and began to rise further and further towards the north-east, and to set further and further towards the north-west. Without proper reverence and ceremonial appeasement the sun might decide to continue on its ever diminishing course at its south-easterly rising and south-westerly setting, finally disappearing altogether and plunging the world into perpetual cold and darkness.

In addition to the stones of the Sarsen and Bluestone Circles and the Trilithon and Bluestone Horseshoes, there are several other features for the visitor to see. One is the Altar Stone, lying flat inside the curve of the Trilithon Horseshoe, and the Slaughter Stone, also lying on its face, near the north-east entrance. Outside the entrance is the Avenue, a corridor flanked by two parallel banks and ditches, running north-eastwards from Stonehenge, and then curving to the east and then to the south to join the River Avon.

The dates when these individual components of Stonehenge were set up are not known for certain, which makes it difficult to establish the sequence. Improved dating techniques that have been developed over the last couple of decades have pushed the establishment of the various features at Stonehenge further and further back in time. As the landscape historian Professor W. G. Hoskins said, everything is older than you think, so it is likely that in the future there will be further revisions regarding the timescale and the sequence of the parts of Stonehenge, perhaps pushing its origins further back into prehistory.

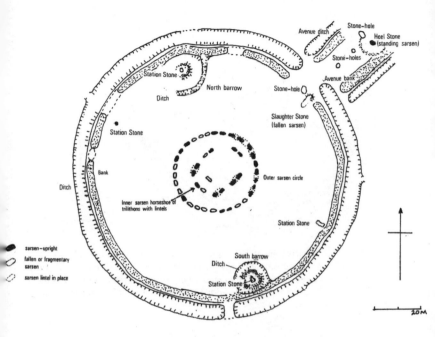

Fig. 11. The Sarsen Circle and the Trilithon Horseshoe as first planned, without the later addition of the smaller Bluestones. The features shown on this plan may not have been built at the same time. It is certain that the Sarsen Circle replaced the Double Bluestone Circle, around 2450 BC, but the Four Station Stones set close to the outer bank, forming an almost perfect rectangle, were probably already in situ, framing the Double Bluestone Circle possibly about 50 years after it was set up. Two of the Four Station Stones were surrounded at a later time by a bank and ditch, interpreted as barrows and labelled as such. The Avenue was probably built last of all, though a late date is not universally accepted. Whether it preceded or post-dated the Sarsen Circle, the Avenue was not precisely matched up to the opening of the north-east entrance, which was narrower that the processional way leading up to it, and slightly offset from it. The bank and ditch of the circle had to be cut back so that the entrance could be widened to match the Avenue. The alignment of the whole monument was now changed, allowing for a more precise observation of the midsummer sunrise, and possibly converting the lunar observatory to a solar one. Drawn by Jacqui Taylor after Darvill 2007.

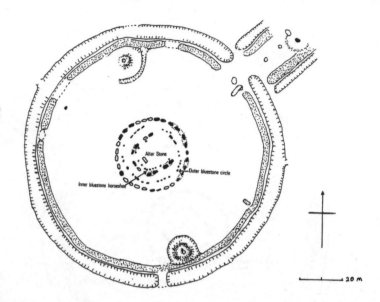

Fig. 12. After the construction of the Sarsen Circle and the Trilithon Horseshoe the shorter Bluestones were brought back to line the inner faces of the Circle and Horseshoe. There is some debate and the dates when the Four Station Stones and the Avenue at the north-east entrance were added to the monument. Drawn by Jacqui Taylor after Darvill 2007.

Preparing the site

Archaeological evidence shows that the Bluestones of the double circle or half-circle were removed carefully. The sockets were deliberately filled in and topped off with white chalk, rather than leaving them open for a time, allowing the edges to crumble inwards and gradually fill in the holes. It was a clearly a conscious decision to dismantle the previous monument and replace it with a bigger and better one. After the removal of the Bluestones, the larger Sarsen Stones were brought to the site, and the Circle and the inner Horseshoe were created. This probably began *c.* 2450 BC, though dates as far apart as 2620 to 2100 BC have been suggested.

The whole procedure, described in so few words, sounds easy. The people took out the earlier stones and brought in different ones, but this process would have required millions of man-hours, and may even have been a long-term project carried out by successive generations of Stonehenge people. The numbers of workers that the project required can only be estimated, and no one can say with any certainty how many men, and possibly women and children, would have been available at any one time to transport the stones, shape and smooth them, dig the sockets for them, and erect them. It is usually assumed that planting and harvesting would have interrupted the work, but it is also possible that there was sufficient food and a surplus of population to create a permanent workforce whose members worked most of the time, at least during all the months from spring to autumn, supported and supplied by the remaining people. Even so, the creation of Stonehenge would have extended over many years.

Transporting the stones

The provenance of the Sarsen Stones that were used to build the circle and the Trilithon Horseshoe is not as hotly debated as that of the Bluestones. The Sarsen Stones weigh several tons, and being one of the hardest stones, they are not easy to shape and smooth, but at least they did not have to be transported for hundreds of miles. The most likely location for these stones, not necessarily their geological origin, was the Marlborough Downs, east and south of Avebury, where in some places large boulders are still visible on the ground surface, brought there by glacial action in the remote past.

Each stone of the finished Stonehenge would have to be transported southwards to the site where they were to be set up. Three different routes have been proposed, some scholars favouring a riverside route following the course of the Avon, while others prefer more westerly routes, the outer one swinging out past what would eventually become Devizes, and approaching Stonehenge from the west, and the inner one, between this outer route and the river, approaching the monument from the north-west after surmounting the slope of Redhorn Hill. There is no absolute proof for any of these proposed routes.

The stones would have to be hauled for a distance of 20 to 30 miles (32 to 48 kilometres), depending on the route chosen. The use of rollers and sledges has already been discussed in connection with the transport of the Bluestones, but it is worth considering two other suggestions as to how the stones may have been brought to Stonehenge. A recent theory, tested in a practical trial, is that the ubiquitous Neolithic rounded stone balls, of astonishingly equal proportions, that have been found on prehistoric sites may have been used like ball bearings, set inside a hardwood conduit, the top half of which would slide along the bottom half with the aid of the stone bearings. Two parallel tracks could be laid in this way, and then the Sarsen Stones could be loaded onto platforms on top. This was shown on a television programme and had mixed results. As weights were increased, the wood chosen for the hollowed trackways was crushed, but with lesser weights (much less than the average Sarsen Stone) the experiment showed that only a few people were needed to pull a few tons quite rapidly along the trackways. It is an ingenious suggestion that still cannot be proven, but because the weights that were transported during the experiment did not approach the tonnage of even the smallest of the Sarsens, the question of prehistoric transport remains open.

Another theory derives from ancient Egyptian evidence, and has not been tried out to test its practicality in Britain. Once again this is evidence from another country and another time slot, but it still belongs to an era before the use of metals and the invention of wheeled transport. While he was investigating the Pyramids, Professor Flinders Petrie noted the presence in model form of the tools used in building the structures. Some of these are in the Cairo Museum. Among them were objects that were best described as cradles, consisting of two pieces of wood with one curved edge and one straight edge, like half-moons, joined by wooden pegs set just inside the edges of the curved sides. These are quarter circles, which Petrie thought would have been used to tilt the stones into position, but Dick Parry (*Engineering the Pyramids*, Sutton 2004) suggested that they may have been used for transporting the stones. Eight of these cradles could have been fixed round the stones, four at each end, to make a complete circle at both ends, and then the stones could be rolled. Like the Neolithic people of Britain, the Egyptians had only stone tools, and whilst the wheel had not been invented in Neolithic Britain, the construction of such cradles would not be beyond the techniques of the carpenters.

Trials conducted in Tokyo showed that properly smoothed rectangular stones presented no problems, but the cradles could also be used on stones with uneven surfaces, by using wooden packing to fill the gaps between the rough edges of the stones and the cradles. The Tokyo experiments proved that in equipping stones of 2.5 metric tons with eight cradles, only a few men were required to lever up the ends of the stones onto a centrally placed base, which left the ends free of the ground and allowed the fitting of the lower cradles, then the other three could be applied at each end. All four were tightly roped together. The fact that the struts joining the two sides of wood were set lower than the edges suggests that provision was made for ropes to be coiled around them. Set inside the eight cradles the stones could be rolled very easily on a flat surface. If the dimensions of the stones and the surrounding cradles were not the same, even with packing, so that the cradles did not form a true circle, the stones could still be rolled, albeit a little more jerkily. Changes of direction could be achieved by levering one side round until the stone on its cradles faced the right way.

In the Tokyo experiment, two tracks were provided, one of lightly compacted gravel and another of heavily compacted gravel, and it was found that the cradles performed well on both tracks, with only two or three men pushing the stones. On slopes, ropes were coiled around the cradles, and the blocks of stone could be hauled up by about ten to fifteen men depending on the angle of the slope. 525 feet or 160 metres of rope were coiled round the cradles, which would enable the men hauling the stones to move for half that distance, since for every 2 metres of rope paid out the stones would move for 1 metre. A wooden chock held the cradles, with their load of 2.5 tonnes, perfectly still on a slope of 1 in 4.

For several reasons the relevance of this experiment to Stonehenge may be considered to be minimal, since no great knowledge is required to point out that the Sarsen Stones of Stonehenge weighed very much more than most of the blocks used to build the Pyramids, but the principle is sound. If the heaviest Sarsen Stones did not crush a sledge, which is advocated as a means of moving them, they probably would not crush four cradles placed on their ends. The experiment was conducted with the intention of illustrating how the builders of the Egyptian pyramids moved their stones, and it is taken as read that they used ramps, so the use of ropes to haul the stones inside their cradles was necessary. The Neolithic people moving the stones towards Stonehenge could have been faced by slopes, depending on which route they used, but none would be as steep as 1 in 4, as in the Tokyo experiments. However, the Neolithic people did know how to make ropes. The plant fibre ones that they used for everyday purposes would not have been strong enough to pull heavy stones, but it is suggested that they wound together strips of leather to make much stronger ropes, and it is taken as read that they must have pulled sledges using ropes such as these.

The use of cradles is only one more suggestion among many as to how to move large heavy stones, and it is no more of a crackpot idea to mention it here as a possible method that might have been used at Stonehenge. There is no evidence for the use of cradles, no tracks, nothing that could support the theory, but then there is nothing for any of the other suggestions either.

None of the haulage methods proposed by modern archaeologists would have been very stable, and all of them would have been challenged by marshy ground, uneven surfaces, and low hills; but like the Bluestones, somehow the Sarsens arrived at Stonehenge, demonstrating incredible determination on the part of the prehistoric people who built the monument. Whatever the method that was chosen, it is possible that oxen would be used for pulling the stones, since the pulling power of one ox is several times greater than that of a man.

Preparing the stones

The stones may have been partially shaped into rectangular blocks before they were transported to the site, which would reduce the weight to be hauled. At Stonehenge itself, Sarsen chippings were found, either near to, or underneath, the bank of the Avenue at the north-east entrance, suggesting that a lot of the work of shaping the stones was done in that vicinity. From the excavation report it is unfortunately not clear precisely where the chippings were found, thus impeding any attempt to demonstrate that the bank and ditch of the Avenue were laid out on top of the debris left there after the stones were shaped.

At the beginning of the twentieth century, Sarsen Stone mauls were found at Stonehenge, varying considerably in size and weight. Some of them were small enough to be held in the hand, but others weighed up to 66 pounds (30 kilos), so it is thought that these would be encased in a sling, probably of leather, and wielded by more than one man to swing against the large stones and pound them until sections broke off. Sarsens are marginally harder than steel, so converting the boulders into the roughly rectangular blocks that we see today would have taken countless hours of pounding and smoothing. When the shape was achieved, and the four sides sufficiently worn down, gangs of people would smooth them by rubbing them with hand-held Sarsen mauls, scraping back and forth along the stones to remove infinitesimal layers off the surface. This would eventually produce shallow gullies and ridges, and then the ridges would be flattened in the same way. One of the stones still displays these gullies and ridges, suggesting that work on smoothing it stopped for some reason. Possibly this represents the earliest-known industrial strike action. The work must have been very boring, but it is not known for how long any individual would have worked on the smoothing process. It is noted that the sides of the stones facing inwards were smoothed off much more efficiently than the backs, involving many more hours to produce the desired finish, and suggesting that whatever ceremonials were carried out inside the monument automatically incurred a sense of respect for the appearance of the stones.

While some gangs were involved in stone shaping, others would have to mark out and dig the sockets for the finished products to be placed inside and erected. If, as seems likely, the Station Stones were already in place, the diagonals could be used to find the centre of the circle. A stake was probably planted at this point, and a rope swung round to mark out the circle, and more stakes planted to mark the places where the thirty stones were to be set. Then the Trilithon Horseshoe could be marked facing the north-east entrance. Neither this suggested method, nor the sequence, is immutable, though naturally it would not have been possible to mark out the circle if the Horseshoe was already marked out, even if this entailed simply planting some stakes, and marking the circle would certainly not have been possible if the Trilithon Horseshoe had been erected.

Erecting the stones

Preparing the stones ready for lifting into their sockets was a process that would probably have taken months rather than weeks for each one. Some of the stones could have been placed in position while further stones were being shaped and smoothed. The building sequence is not known, but it is likely that the stones of the Trilithon Horseshoe were erected first to avoid having to drag them in through the relatively narrow gaps of the completed Sarsen Circle. Work on both the circle and the Horseshoe may have been carried out at the same time, with a large gap being left for access through the circle, which would then be completed when the Trilithons were in place. It must be acknowledged that these theories do not meet with universal acceptance, and a dating sequence has been proposed which puts the completion of the circle as much as two or three centuries before the erection of the Horseshoe.

The sockets for the upright stones were dug with one side sloping inwards and the other three sides vertical. The theory is that the stones would be pushed on rollers with what would be its bottom end facing towards the socket, then weights would be put onto the end to assist its tilt into the socket where it would rest at an angle supported by the sloping side. Then it would be hauled upright, coming to a halt against the opposite vertical face, which may have been lined with timbers as a buffer to prevent the weight of the stone from crushing the soil. As the stone rose it could have been supported at the rear by timber posts to prevent it from falling back, though putting these timbers into place may have been a hazardous occupation. The trick would have been to prevent the stones from tilting too far forward after it had dropped into the socket, though modern experiments using concrete uprights were not troubled by this potential mishap. When it was in place, the standing stone would be packed round with smaller stones and earth.

For the Trilithon Horseshoe this procedure would have to be performed ten times, and for the circle thirty times. When the uprights were in place and secured, the lintels would be raised onto the uprights. Various suggestions for how this was done include building a ramp of earth close up to each set of uprights and hauling the stone up the slope, or placing timber beams at an angle from the ground to the top of the stones and binding the lintels with ropes, then hauling them up by teams working from the other side, which would give modern health and safety inspectors a few headaches. The favoured method, reproduced in several books, involves the creation of a timber platform all around the uprights, with the lintels mounted on top and raised one side at a time for the insertion of more timbers, until the top of the uprights was reached. Then the lintel could be dragged into place. If such a timber platform was used, the logs would probably have been squared off for greater stability, since tree trunks would be subject to a greater degree of movement unless they were pegged. There is no evidence for such pegging, nor for any of the other methods of raising the lintels, because there would be hardly any trace on the ground even when the tasks were carried out, much less thousands of years later. The advantage of using timber platforms would be that the logs could be disassembled and used for the next platform.

The lintels were not simply placed on top of the uprights, but were secured by means of mortice and tenon joints like those used in carpentry, and already familiar to the prehistoric builders of Stonehenge. The tops of the uprights were shaped, the edges chipped away to leave a smooth area all around and a tenon poking up in the middle. The corresponding lintels had two depressions made in them, to form the mortices, matching the size and spacing of the tenons of the two uprights for which the lintel was destined. There was no exact standardisation of design in either size or shape. Stonehenge was not like modern flat-pack furniture, so the lintels could not be manufactured en masse. Neither the width of the paired Trilithon stones, nor the gaps between them, were exactly the same, so each lintel for the Trilithons had to be tailor-made, to match the dimensions of the pair of uprights, not protruding beyond the edges, and not falling short, as well as exactly matching the tenon joints. For the Sarsen Circle, the same principles applied but here the lintels were even more sophisticated. The lintels had to fit only halfway along each of its uprights, instead of spanning a complete separate pair like the lintels of the Trilithons. Each lintel was slightly curved to retain the circular formation, and each one had not only two mortices in its underside, but also a tongue

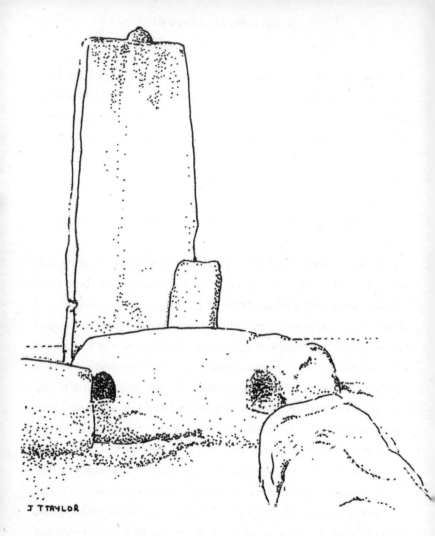

J TTAYLOR

Fig. 13. Drawing of the central Trilithon Stone 56, the tallest stone of the whole monument, showing the tenon at the top of the stone. In front of it is one of the Bluestones, and in front of that there is the fallen lintel Stone 156 with its two mortice holes. This lintel was originally placed on top of Stones 55 and 56, but Stone 55 fell down and broke up, bringing the lintel Stone 156 with it. Both still lie on the ground. The reason for the collapse was the fact that Stone 55 was much shorter than its partner Stone 56, so in order to bring it to the same height as Stone 56 and ensure that the lintel 156 would be level, it had to be set in a shallower socket, only four feet deep as opposed to the eight-foot socket of Stone 56. The prehistoric builders tried to compensate for the shallow socket by carving a projecting foot at the bottom of Stone 55 to anchor it more firmly, but it fell down eventually, pinning down the Altar Stone in the curve of the Horseshoe. The fall also caused Stone 56 to tilt at a considerable angle which increased dramatically as time went on. It continued to lean ever more earthwards until it was brought back to the vertical in the 1950s. Drawn by Jacqui Taylor.

and groove arrangement at the ends, so that each lintel would not only lock onto the tenon joints of the uprights, but would also lock into its neighbouring lintels. There were some mistakes, either accidental or deliberate. One lintel had two sets of mortices on both sides, as though the first arrangement had failed to match its uprights, and two stones had a tongue at each end instead of one tongue and a corresponding groove.

One of the most amazing features of the stones of the Horseshoe and the Circle is the careful adjustment of their levels. The Trilithons are not all of the same height, but adjusted so that the two arms sit successively lower towards the north-east entrance, while the pair of stones at the south-west end, in the enclosed part of the Horseshoe, tower above the whole monument. The Sarsen Circle is built on uneven ground with a gradual slope from the west to the east, and a much shallower slope from south to north, but the uprights and lintels of the circle are all level. This would entail finding stones of more or less the correct height for whichever part of the Horseshoe or Circle it was destined, and also digging deeper or shallower sockets to achieve the desired effect. There may have been preliminary trials using wooden posts, to make a timber mock-up, but this cannot be proven.

In order to ensure that the lintels were level, a prehistoric version of a modern spirit level could have been used, by placing a vessel containing water on top of the lintels. If there was even a small variation in the level, the water would run to one end of its container, but if the surface was flat, water would overflow evenly all around the container. But it is one thing to know if a surface is level and quite another to achieve it. The height of each upright had to be measured and the depth of its socket adjusted accordingly, a bald statement that ignores the blood, toil, tears

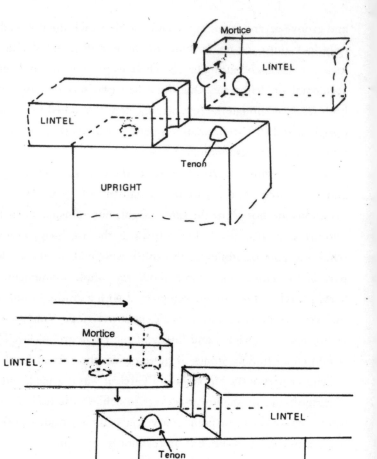

Fig. 14. Diagram showing how the lintels of the Sarsen Circle fitted on top of the uprights by means of a hollowed out mortice, and how they were joined together by a tongue and groove arrangement. Drawn by Jacqui Taylor.

1. A glance at any of the other stone circles in Britain clearly reveals the unique complexity and sophistication of Stonehenge. This is not to denigrate the effort of planning, transport and labour that went into the other stone circles, but the stones were not shaped and smoothed, few of them are as tall as those at Stonehenge, and there are no lintels. This photo shows the circle at Castlerigg near Keswick, Cumbria, in its spectacular setting on a more or less level platform surrounded by mountains. The single circle of unshaped stones is slightly flattened on the north-east side, and slightly peaked at the north where the main entrance lies, flanked by two massive rounded boulders, as seen in this photo. Inside the circle, just visible on the left, is the small rectangular enclosure marked out by large stones.

2. North-east of Penrith, Cumbria, lies the stone circle called Long Meg and Her Daughters. This circle is very large, enclosed by many stones that legend says can never be properly counted. The problem is compounded by the fact that not all the stones of the original circuit are still in situ, and several of the ones that remain are almost buried. The main entrance is in the south-west, where two stones on the south side of the passageway are still visible. These two were once paired on the opposite side, forming an impressive portal of four standing stones. Outside this entrance is Long Meg herself, a tall standing stone of red sandstone with carvings of spirals and concentric circles, similar to the cup and ring marks to be found on many prehistoric sites in the British Isles. The focus here is on the midwinter sunset, marked by Long Meg viewed from inside the circle. The photo shows part of the arc of the circle from the south to the south-west, where Long Meg can be seen protruding above the other stones.

Above: 3. Aerial view of Stonehenge from the north-west. Only three of the five Trilithons are still standing with their lintels, and only the four Sarsen uprights (Stones 29, 30, 1 and 2) facing the north-east entrance still support a continuous run of lintels (130, 101, 102). Outside the stone circle, part of the encircling bank and ditch can be seen in this photo. The small standing stone near the perimeter is Station Stone 93, and the smaller circular bank and ditch further on to the right of it surrounds the place where Station Stone 94 used to stand. From this partial view of the bank and ditch it is clear that the stone circle occupies only a small central area in what started out as a much larger enclosure. Copyright English Heritage Photo Library.

Opposite top: 4. This view from outside the Sarsen Circle shows the encircling bank and ditch of the earlier versions of Stonehenge. Trilithon Stones 57 and 58 with lintel 158, restored to its present position in the 1950s, is visible right of centre through a gap in the Sarsen Circle. Copyright Sacred Destinations.

Opposite bottom: 5. Stonehenge seen from the west on a grey and cloudy day. At the extreme right of the photo the people standing next to Sarsen 16 provide an idea of scale. Sarsen 16 stands alone, bereft of its companions on the west and south-west.

6. Even on a bright day the stones of Stonehenge can seem somewhat enclosed and claustrophobic. This view is taken looking towards the south-east. On the right of the picture can be seen the only complete Trilithon on the west side, with its lintel (Stones 57 and 58 and lintel 158). Further to the right of the photo are Sarsens 21 and 22 with lintel 122. Through the gap where no Sarsens remain standing the single Trilithon (Stone 60) can be seen, with its tenon visible at the top. Its partner Stone 59, and the lintel 160 both lie flat beside it. Beyond these there are Trilithons of the east side, Stones 51 and 52 with lintel 152, and Stones 53 and 54 with lintel 154. Copyright Sacred Destinations.

7. This view across part of the bank and ditch shows how compact the stone monument is compared to the original extent of the first version of Stonehenge. The taller stones of the Trilithons can be seen protruding above the tops of the remaining Sarsens. Just visible lying on the ground is a fallen Sarsen (Stone 8), and Sarsens 4 and 5 with lintel 105, and Sarsens 6 and 7 with lintel 107, but the lintel 106 that would have joined the two has fallen down. Copyright Sacred Destinations.

8. On the east, south and west sectors of the Sarsen Circle, many of the stones have fallen down or have disappeared altogether, leaving large gaps, as shown in this photo. The tall single upright in the middle of the photo is Trilithon Stone 56, and standing behind it in isolation is Sarsen Stone 16. The absence of many of the Sarsens has led to the theory that the Sarsen Circle was never completed.

9. This view of Sarsen Stone 16 on the right and Trilithon Stone 56 on the left shows how open the monument is at this point, with a marked lack of pairs of Sarsens with lintels. There are not enough fallen stones to account for the conjectured missing upright and lintels.

Above: 10. The wide gaps on the south and south east of the Sarsen Circle can be seen in this photo. The shorter stone leaning outwards is Sarsen Stone 11. It is thought that the builders of Stonehenge deliberately used this shorter stone, rather than choosing one of the same height as the other uprights. There may have been a wooden superstructure on top of this stone to bring it in line with the other Sarsens.

Below: 11. A tour round the Sarsen Circle offers a different prospect every few feet. Not many uprights still retain their lintels, the two shown here being Stones 21 and 22 with lintel 122, and to the right of these is Stone 23, standing alone. Stone 24 is missing.

12. Oblique view of Sarsen Stones 21 and 22 with their lintel 122, showing how the lintels cover only half of the uprights, leaving room on either side for adjoining lintels. Nowadays these stones are the only ones in the western half of the monument to possess a lintel. Stone 23 survives on its own, and all of the uprights and lintels between Stone 16 and Stone 21 have disappeared.

Left: 13. Given the right sort of weather, all the stones of Stonehenge are extremely photogenic. This photo shows Stones 22 and 23 with lintel 122, as seen from the inside of the Sarsen Circle.

Below: 14. The four uprights of the Sarsen Circle with a continuous run of lintels (Stones 29, 30, 1 and 2, facing the north-east entrance to the monument). This photo is taken through a gap in the Sarsen Circle, with Stones 27 and 28 at the extreme left.

Opposite, top: 15. This photo shows how narrow were the gaps between the Sarsens of the stone circle, creating an atmosphere of exclusion as seen from the outside, and seclusion inside the monument. The two stones with protrusions facing outwards at the tops, one with resident crow facing the camera, are Sarsens 27 and 28. Inside the curve of the circle some of the smaller and shorter stones of the inner Bluestone circle can be seen. The two furthest Bluestones (Stones 49 and 31), paired with the Sarsens (Stones 30 and 1) are set on either side of the north-east alignment, and at the midsummer sunrise these stones frame the rising sun. Copyright Sacred Destinations.

16. Sarsen Stone 28 with its upper bulge facing the camera, and the first part of the curve formed by Stones 29, 30, 1 and 2, seen from outside the Sarsen Circle.

17. The extent and size of the Sarsen Circle can be gauged from this view of Stones 29, 30, 1 and 2, framing the north-east entrance. Some of the remaining Bluestones are also visible, forming part of the inner Bluestone Circle, smaller than the Sarsens and a later addition to the monument.

18. The Sarsen Circle viewed from the inside. Stones 29, 30, 1 and 2 can be seen, together with solitary Stone 3 and Stones 4 and 5 with lintel. The shorter Bluestones line the inner circuit. With a visitor to provide scale, it can be seen how massive the Sarsens are.

19. Sarsen Stones 29, 30, 1 and 2, joined together with a run of three lintels, seen from the outside of the Circle, showing how exclusive the whole monument would have seemed when it was complete.

Left: 20. Sarsen Stone 30 and 29 and a glimpse of protruding Stone 28, viewed from outside the Circle, in picturesque mode.

Above right: 21. View towards the north taken from the inside of the Sarsen Circle, looking over fallen Sarsens, to Bluestones 49 and 31, which mark the narrow opening of the circle facing the north-east entrance. Copyright Sacred Destinations.

22. In the foreground, one of the Bluestones of the inner Circle, framed by Sarsen Stones 29, 30, 1 and 2 at the north-east entrance.

23. An exterior view of the Sarsen Circle viewed from the north-east, the view that would have faced Neolithic and Bronze Age visitors coming in from the Avenue.

24. The Bluestones and Sarsens at the north-east, viewed from inside the monument.

25. Dead centre between Sarsen Stone 1 on the left and Stone 30 on the right, the remaining upright of the tallest Trilithon of the Horseshoe can be seen, with its distinctive tenon. This is Trilithon Stone 56, now minus its partner Stone 55 which lies recumbent beside it.

26. As part of the ongoing repairs to Stonehenge that were begun in the twentieth century, Trilithon Stone 57 and 58 and lintel 158 were re-erected using modern lifting gear, as shown in this photo. To the right of the Trilithon undergoing reconstruction is Trilithon 56 with its tenon clearly seen projecting from the top. It stands alone, as it has done since its partner Stone 55 fell down. The fall dragged Stone 56 out of the vertical, causing it to tilt forwards at an ever sharper angle as time went on. Drawings made prior to the twentieth century show this stone almost ready to topple over. By the time this photo was taken in 1958 Stone 56 had been pulled back to its upright position, and secured in concrete, a useful invention of the Romans and entirely unknown to prehistoric people. Copyright English Heritage Photo Library.

27. On the left of this photo taken from the south can be seen Stone 56 with its tenon projecting from the top. Together with Stone 55 and lintel 156, both now lying on the ground, Stone 56 formed the tallest Trilithon at the curve of the Horseshoe. Before Stone 55 and the lintel fell down, the midwinter sunset would have been seen between the two uprights, through the gap between the lintel 156 and the lower lintel of the Sarsen Circle behind it. The upright Trilithon stones and their lintel, and the lower lintel of the Sarsen Circle behind it would frame the setting sun in a sort of rectangular window, similar to the roof box of the tomb at Newgrange in Ireland, which admitted the rising midwinter sun into the passage between the burial chambers. Copyright Sacred Destinations.

28. From the outside of the Circle it can be difficult to distinguish the Trilithons of the Horseshoe from the few remaining Sarsen pairs with lintels, even though the Trilithons are taller than the Sarsens. A closer examination reveals that the Trilithon lintels cover the exact width of both the uprights, whereas the Sarsen lintels are placed only half way over each upright in order to join with their neighbours.

29. Both pairs of Trilithons on the east side of the Horseshoe are still standing. These are Stones 54 and 53 with lintel 154, viewed from inside the Sarsen Circle, and further along Stone 52 and the end of lintel 152 obscure Stone 51.

30. Trilithon Stones 53 and 54 and lintel 154 from inside the Horseshoe. This photo shows how carefully the Stones were worked and smoothed, and how the lintels were beautifully squared off, by people using only stone tools, around three thousand years ago.

31. As it moves round to the west, the sun casts the shadow of Trilithon Stone 56 over Trilithons 53 and 54.

Left: 33. At the closed end of the Horseshoe stood the tallest of the five Trilithons, now sadly broken. Stone 56 stands alone next to its fallen partner Stone 55. One of the Bluestones of the inner Horseshoe, sloping at an angle towards Trilithon Stones 57 and 58, has a groove along its side, possibly indicating that in a former scheme it was linked to other Bluestones by the tongue and groove method, though this must remain conjectural.

Opposite: 32. Two of the Bluestones of the inner Horseshoe that lined the taller Trilithon Horseshoe, one sky-lined, and to its right the other one seen against Trilithon Stone 53.

34. A closer view of the Bluestone with its side groove, which cannot have been created by a natural phenomenon, so it must have been deliberately carved, serving some function about which modern archaeologists can only guess.

35. Here it can be seen how the tallest Trilithon, represented only by Stone 56 at the rear of the Horseshoe, directly faced the north-east entrance, framed by the Sarsen Stones 29, 30, visible here, with Stones 1 and 2 out of view, just off the right-hand edge of the photo.

36. Viewed from inside the Sarsen Circle, Trilithon Stones 57 and 58, as restored in the 1950s, with the grooved Bluestone almost in front of it, and just beyond them are Trilithon Stones 53 and 54, forming the eastern arm of the Horseshoe, which like the western arm gradually reduces in height towards the open end at the north-east.

38. A dizzying view taken from the base of Trilithon 57 and 58, looking up at lintel 158, which shows how tall and massive these stones are, and highlights the tremendous engineering task their transport, shaping and erection posed to the Neolithic builders.

Opposite: 37. Trilithons 57 and 58 photographed as the sun moves round towards the west. The shadow of Sarsen Stone 21 and half of lintel 122 can be seen on the left hand upright.
Above: 39. This view into the Horseshoe, showing the Trilithons and one of the Bluestones, suggests how potentially claustrophobic and exclusive Stonehenge must have been. Was this a view restricted to a few specially authorised people?

40. The gaps between the uprights of the Trilithons were very narrow, for reasons unknown, but the restricted viewing slots have been used to bolster the theories that Stonehenge was used for astronomical sightings.

41. Whether or not Stonehenge
was a solar, lunar or
astronomical observatory, it has
to be admitted that this sort of
view possesses an extraordinary
ambience.

Above: 42. The carved features on some of the Trilithons and other stones were discovered quite recently. These daggers on Trilithon Stone 53 are very similar to actual Bronze Age examples, but the full significance of the carvings remains unknown. There are also several axe heads on Stone 53, and other carvings have been found on Sarsen Stones 3, 4, 5, 23, 29 and 30, and on Trilithons 55 and 57.

Left: 43. When does vandalism metamorphose into historical documentary evidence? Modern humans tend to carve their initials or their names rather than daggers and axes.

44. A close view of the tenon on Trilithon Stone 56, one of the uprights of the tallest of the Trilithons. The mortice holes of the corresponding lintel that once joined Stone 56 with the fallen Stone 55 would have had to be carved to the exact dimensions to fit over the tenons.

45. Wear and tear on this lintel reveals the tenon underneath.

Above: 46. The recumbent stone in the foreground shows the grooves and ridges created by the long patient smoothing process, carried out by rubbing stone mauls along the surface until the Sarsen stones were shaped. On the other stones the ridges were smoothed away, but the people who worked on this stone seem to have abandoned the task before it was finished. *Below*: 48. View of the Heel Stone from inside the Sarsen Circle. It is framed on the left by Sarsen Stone 30 with Bluestone 49 in front of it, and on the right by Sarsen Stone 1 and Bluestone 31. In prehistoric times the midsummer sun would have risen between the existing Heel Stone and its now vanished partner to its left.

47. The famous Heel Stone, once upright but leaning slightly after many centuries. Its former partner stone has vanished, only detectable now by the archaeological traces of its slot in the ground.

Above: 49. The Heel Stone seen from the inner edge of the Sarsen Circle, with the shadow of one of the Bluestones of the inner Circle on the right hand Sarsen upright.

Opposite: 50. The so-called Slaughter Stone outside the Sarsen Circle, near the north-east entrance. It was given this lurid description by antiquarians who imagined grisly sacrifices at Stonehenge. However, it would have been difficult to slaughter someone on this stone, because it once stood upright, and had companions that may have defined a monumental entrance to Stonehenge.

51. The so-called Avenue is a processional way to or from the north-east entrance. The remains of the parallel banks and ditches that flanked it are clearly visible from the air, but on the ground they are much harder to see. This photo demonstrates how observant William Stukeley was, in discerning the Avenue from scant traces on the ground.

52. Stones and sky at Stonehenge, an eternal combination. This monument is not only unimaginably ancient, it is unique, and while there are many fantastic monuments in Wales, Scotland, Ireland and the rest of Europe, this particular one is in England.

and sweat that would undoubtedly have been involved in handling several tons of Sarsen Stone.

This careful adjustment of height is demonstrated very well by the two largest Trilithons, at the closed end of the Horseshoe, Stones 55 and 56 in the current numbering scheme. One of these uprights, Stone 55, with its accompanying lintel, fell down and broke at some unknown date, perhaps even in prehistoric times. A sixteenth-century drawing of the site shows that the upright and the lintel had already fallen across the Altar Stone by then. Perhaps at the time when its partner and the lintel fell, Stone 56 keeled over slightly. At the beginning of the twentieth century it had begun to lean rather perilously towards the inside of the monument. It was straightened up and secured by setting it in concrete.

Investigation of the two massive stones revealed that Stone 56, which survived the catastrophe when its neighbour and its lintel fell down, was set at least 8 feet (2.4 metres) into the ground, whereas Stone 55 was shorter; to make the tops of the two uprights level, the socket for Stone 55 had to be much shallower, at about 4 feet (1.2 metres), therefore Stone 55 was sunk into the ground at only half the depth of Stone 56. In order to compensate for this precarious setting, the base of Stone 55 had been shaped with a projecting foot in an attempt to anchor it more firmly.

All this, the transport and shaping of the stones, the levelling of the circle and its lintels and the gradual slope of the Trilithon Horseshoe, is precision engineering, late Neolithic/early Bonze Age style. Both the concept and its execution are staggering, and ought to induce what is colloquially termed the wow factor.

The Altar Stone

The purpose of this stone, lying flat inside the Trilithon Horseshoe, was decided by antiquarians who saw Stonehenge as a place of sacrifice, possibly human. In reality the function of the so-called Altar Stone is not known. Debate centres round its recumbent position, some scholars preferring to interpret it as a former standing stone, perhaps with a partner, at the closed end of the Horseshoe, while another group suggests that it had always been laid flat. Before the Sarsen Circle was built, the Altar Stone was a standing stone at the side of the Double Bluestone Circle, or half-circle. Then it was moved to the inside of the Trilithon Horseshoe, whether as a standing or recumbent stone, though on balance it is most likely that it was placed flat on the ground from the very start.

In its present position, the Altar Stone is very nearly aligned across the central curve of the Horseshoe, but not quite. It projects slightly further to the west across the main alignment than it does to the east, so it is not precisely central. Lying across the north-east–south-west alignment, the Altar Stone was probably intended to form a right angle with the axis, but it is a few degrees short of the 90 degrees that would be required. Given the weight and size of the Altar Stone, and the shortcomings of the otherwise awe-inspiring prehistoric technology, these are minor quibbles. It has to be acknowledged that the chances of the Altar Stone arriving by accident at this so nearly central position are minimal. At some time in prehistory or later, the Altar Stone was pinned down by the fallen and broken Trilithon Stone 55 and the lintel belonging to it and its partner Stone 56, so it has been suggested that when this upright fell down, it knocked the once upright Altar Stone to the ground. Aubrey Burl points out that if this is what happened, then

Fig. 15. Reconstruction drawing of the finished monument, showing a complete circle of Sarsen Stones joined by their lintels, and the taller Trilithon Horseshoe, larger at the enclosed end and tapering downwards at the open ends. The Bluestones can be seen lining the two parts of the monument, and the Altar Stone lies across the closed end of the Trilithon Horseshoe. Drawn by Jacqui Taylor after Janet and Colin Bord.

the Altar Stone would probably not have fallen over in its current position, certainly not at such an almost central position at right angles to the axis. The most logical assumption, if the Altar Stone had been a standing stone and had been knocked down by the falling Trilithon, is that it ought to have fallen forwards and should now be lying on the ground pointing towards the mouth of the Trilithon and Bluestone Horseshoes. If this is what happened the Altar Stone would have remained trapped there forever, because it would have been impossible to turn it round so that it lay across the curve of the Horseshoe without also moving the broken Stone 55 and its lintel.

Further indications that the Altar Stone was never in an upright position in the Horseshoe derive from the lack of any socket for it. If the Altar Stone had been set into a socket with a sloping ramp, and had fallen down by itself before the Trilithon collapsed, it really ought to have fallen forward against the ramp, because the ground there would have been less resistant than on the other three sides. But there is no evidence that there was ever a socket for the Altar Stone. William Stukeley tried to find one, but discovered that all around the stone there was only compact chalk, so he concluded that it had never been intended to stand upright. As Aubrey Burl also points out, there are only very few stone circles in southern England which have, or had, a standing stone in the centre. Since Stonehenge was always an anomaly among stone circles, the absence of standing stones inside other circles does not constitute hard evidence that the builders of the Trilithon Horseshoe did not place a standing stone inside it. Since there can be no absolute proof as to the original position of the Altar Stone, opinions must be based on pure speculation, but it may be significant that the recumbent stone lies across the sight-line from the inside of the Horseshoe through the gap in the Trilithons to the midwinter sunset. As mentioned above, the setting sun shines through a sort of roof box, framed by the Trilithon uprights Stones 55 and 56, and by the two lintels of the Trilithon itself and the Sarsen Circle. The Altar Stone closes off an arc of the Trilithon Horseshoe, comparable, in a way, to an apse inside a church. On the inner faces of the Trilithons on either side of this arc there are carvings on the Sarsens. Stone 57 on the western side bears a depiction of an axe handle and some figures; and on the east, Stone 53 has a dagger and twelve axes. The date of the carvings and their purpose are unknown, but the Altar Stone, and the area between it and the end of the Horseshoe, may have been especially sacred or powerful, perhaps the preserve of the select few who performed the ceremonies there.

The Avenue

The date when this corridor to the River Avon was established is disputed, as are the dates for all the features of Stonehenge. The Avenue is a modern term for the long stretch of land enclosed by parallel banks and ditches. It may have been started *c.* 2400 BC shortly after the Sarsen Circle was erected, though it has been placed as much as two centuries earlier. It may have been contemporary with the Double Bluestone Circle, but the date of 2400–2300 BC is thought to mark the construction of other similar avenues at different stone circles in the British Isles.

The Avenue was probably built in stages, starting with a straight section leading into, or out of, the north-east entrance. Then it was extended, curving eastwards and southwards towards the River Avon. The bend in its course has acquired the name 'the Elbow'. It has been suggested that the original intention was to lead into

Stonehenge Bottoms, where there was a water course; but when it dried up, the Avenue was extended to meet the river. The second section is less well constructed than the first. Though there is no visible evidence now, there may once have been standing stones lining the Avenue inside the bank and ditch, like the West Kennet Avenue at Avebury, where lines of stones are still to be seen.

The ends of the banks and ditches on either side of the Avenue do not join up with the bank and ditch of the original circle at Stonehenge, but instead there was a gap of about 3 metres between the curved ends of the Avenue ditches and the ditch of the original enclosure. Nor was the Avenue lined up precisely with the gap of the north-east entrance. It was extended further eastwards so that the bank and ditch of Stonehenge protruded into the passageway. The entrance was therefore widened so that it would match the Avenue, which, as Aubrey Burl points out, slightly altered the axis of the whole monument. The alignment was now firmly directed much more precisely towards the midsummer sunrise and the midwinter sunset. If the purpose of Stonehenge had always been to monitor the midsummer sunrise and midwinter sunset from the very beginning, this purpose was now emphasised more than ever. An awful lot of work was involved in achieving this new alignment, so for the several scholars who do not support the astronomical importance of the monument an alternative explanation is to be sought.

The purpose of the Avenue can only be guessed, but it strongly suggests ceremonials and processions to and from the river. It cannot be known how many times per year the route would be used. It could have been for transport of the remains of the dead, ferried down the river to be buried in the banks of the monument, or it could have been to take the ashes of the dead from Stonehenge and throw them into the water. Stonehenge definitely had connections with the dead, as the numerous cremation burials have shown, so it is to be expected that some form of procession and ceremony would be involved. There may have been processions at the rising of the midsummer sun, and/or at the setting of the midwinter sun. There may have been moon festivals as well, though the focus of Stonehenge is assumed to have changed to a solar observatory when the Sarsen Circle and the Trilithon Horseshoe were built.

It has been suggested that the whole monument at Stonehenge, and the Avenue, were associated with a cult of the dead, whose remains were brought to Stonehenge probably from the henge at Durrington Walls to the north (the realm of the living) then carried along the River Avon and then through the Avenue to Stonehenge (the realm of the dead). It has been pointed out that the Avenue was not used so frequently or for so long that it became a sunken way, formed by the passage of many feet, human or animal. Two suggestions have been made to accommodate this evidence. Either the Avenue went out of use quite quickly, or alternatively it may have been used for a long period of time, but only by a select group, leaders, priests, or perhaps shamans, who performed the ceremonies.

The Slaughter Stone and its companions

When the Avenue was built at the north-east entrance, the eastern terminals of the bank and ditch which surrounds the monument were cut back in order to make the entrance passage wider, and at the same time the axis of Stonehenge was altered by a few degrees. Large upright stones were set just inside the bank and ditch, framing the entrance. The Slaughter Stone was one of these portal stones. According to a drawing made in the second half of the sixteenth century, this stone was upright, but by William Stukeley's day, two centuries later, it had fallen down, lying flat as it does now. Stukeley conjectured that there must have been two large uprights forming a portal to the monument. He was proved correct when excavations in the early twentieth century revealed holes where stones had once been set up, but instead of just one hole there were two, both situated to the west of the Slaughter Stone, labelled D and E.

The E hole, roughly 9.8 feet (3 metres) west of the Slaughter Stone contained two antlers, dated to about 2400 BC, which could mean that the entrance portals were set up around the same time as the Sarsen Circle. Another 9.8 feet (3 metres) further west, the D hole was discovered. The three large stones would not have filled the entire entrance and would not have lined up symmetrically with the opening of the Avenue, but there is room for a fourth stone on the eastern side, where there is a gap between the Slaughter Stone and the ends of the bank and ditch of the Avenue and of the surrounding circle. The gap is about 20 feet (6 metres) wide, leaving room for a postulated fourth upright stone, which could have been placed 9.8 feet (3 metres) eastwards of the Slaughter Stone, preserving the same spacing as the other three stones. As yet no excavations have been undertaken so it must remain a highly likely but unproven theory that there were four standing stones across the entrance, and one of them, the Slaughter Stone, remains in situ, but lying on the ground.

Y and Z holes

The components of Stonehenge described above constitute the final version of the monument. Some scholars have expressed doubts that anything that was ever started at Stonehenge was ever fully competed, and that projects petered out through lack of energy or interest before the complete plan had been fulfilled. This opinion contains a covert assumption that modern students of Stonehenge are privy to the details of the original plan. The gaps in the Sarsen Circle, where there are no remains of stones either standing or lying down, illustrate this controversy. Either there were once upright Sarsens in place which have been removed over the centuries, or there were always gaps from the very first. This situation could indeed have arisen because the builders ran out of steam and abandoned the project, or because the plan was to leave gaps at some points, for whatever reasons can be suggested. An unfinished monument would probably not have impeded the ceremonies that went on at Stonehenge, much as some of the medieval cathedrals functioned perfectly well without a nave in some cases or without transepts, or even a roof. In Europe, cathedrals such as Cologne, Ulm and Milan waited from their medieval foundation dates to the nineteenth century for completion, but in all that time religious functions for which they had been originally intended were carried out. There can be no definitive answer to the questions of whether there was a complete Sarsen Circle at Stonehenge, or whether any of its phases were actually finished. It has to be assumed that Stonehenge in all its guises fulfilled the needs of its builders more than adequately for some considerable time. But in the developing Bronze Age, Stonehenge went out of fashion and became redundant, not for the first time in its long life.

After a long period of disuse, it seems that there was an attempt to revive the monument. A series of holes were dug outside the Sarsen Circle, labelled Y and Z holes by archaeologists. Nothing is visible today. There were two circuits of thirty holes, reflecting the thirty Sarsens, the Z holes numbered 1 to 30 being the innermost ring, with the Y holes, possibly dug later than the Z holes, running round

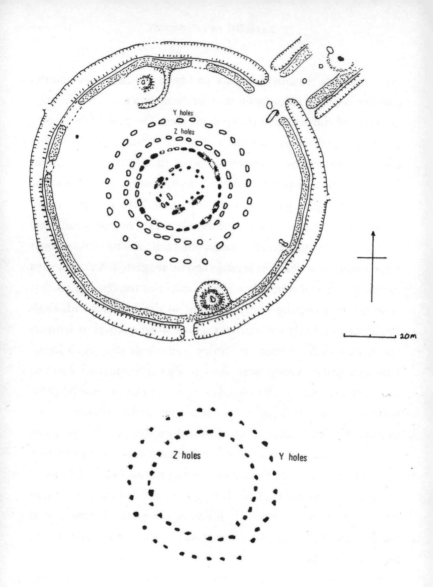

Fig. 16. For an unknown length of time Stonehenge was disused and neglected, until at some time in the Bronze Age someone dug a series of holes in two concentric circles around the outside of the Sarsen Circle. These holes were labelled by archaeologists Y and Z holes, numbered like all other features from 1 to 30 in clockwise fashion from the north-east entrance. The two circles were not properly closed up; both of them show an offset gap in the south, as shown in the lower diagram. The holes were not all dug to the same depth and not all of them were finished. They were intended to mirror the 30 Sarsens, but no-one knows what purpose they served. They probably never held posts, but some of them contained ritual deposits. Drawn by Jacqui Taylor after Darvill 2007.

the outer edge. Antlers from Y30 and Z29 were dated to 1750 BC, but the suggested dates for the two series of holes range from 2030 to 1750 BC for the inner Z holes and 1640 to 1520 BC for the Y holes.

It may have been the intention to form a circle to reflect the Sarsens but there is no evidence that the holes ever supported stones. The holes were not even completed. One of them, Z8, was never even begun, and Y7 was not dug as deeply as the other holes. The circles formed by these holes are somewhat misshapen, since there would be no means of marking out a true circle by means of a peg driven into the ground in the centre and swinging a rope around the circumference. The spacing of the holes is also inaccurate, but perhaps accuracy was not the main aim. Towards the south-east, there seems to have been a deliberate gap, where the holes are slightly offset, but what this means is not ascertained.

The end of Stonehenge

After the creation of the Y and Z holes, it seems that no further modification was carried out at Stonehenge. Times were gradually changing well before this time, as communal burials began to wane and individual burials overlapped and finally superseded the older systems. The use of metals started probably in the mid-third millennium BC, gold ornaments and copper tools preceding the manufacture and use of bronze. Access to metal ornaments, tools and weapons probably underpinned the emergence of individual power, the growth of chiefdoms, and the greater importance of land ownership, and the concomitant factor of all these developments, endemic warfare. The structure of society changed, perhaps older beliefs and rites were replaced by new religious practices, and so the vast circular monument of Stonehenge faded into obsolescence.

Alternative explanations have been suggested. Perhaps it was not just localised changes that sealed the fate of Stonehenge, but worldwide events such as the eruption of the volcano of Santorini in 1628 BC. This major disaster has been linked to the demise of the cities of Crete, and more fantastically to the disappearance of Atlantis, which may have been Santorini itself, or Thera as it then was. More pertinently for Britain, there may have been a long period when the sun was obscured, crops failed and starvation set in. Obviously people survived, but re-emerged in an altered form, in a society that did not need Stonehenge.

7

THE STONEHENGE PEOPLE: LATE NEOLITHIC TO THE END OF THE BRONZE AGE, *c.* 2500 BC TO *c.* 700 BC

The latest phase of Stonehenge was built as the Neolithic way of life was undergoing a slow transformation, merging with the Bronze Age. The names that are bestowed on the eras of prehistory usefully divide the thousands of years into more manageable chunks, but they give a false impression that the process of change between one era and another was sudden and rapid. There was no sharply discernible point in time when the late Neolithic became the early Bronze Age. Just as the Mesolithic era melded with the early Neolithic over a protracted period of time, the Bronze Age did not suddenly emerge fully fledged as the Neolithic came to a shuddering halt. For this reason, archaeologists now refer to the long transition period by the initials LNEBA, late Neolithic/early Bronze Age, giving it an almost separate existence between the age of stone and the final flourishing of the age of bronze tools and weapons, when the use of iron finally took over.

The first known use of metals in Britain coincided with the building of Stonehenge but did not become widespread for a few centuries. Stone and flint weapons and tools continued in use side by side with the growing manufacture of metal versions, and were probably never entirely superseded. Although it was a slow and gradual process, the use of metals heralded changes in society that are visible in the archaeological record. Gold and copper objects and ornaments were manufactured before the use of bronze became more common. On the Continent the use of copper persisted for long enough to merit a name for the period, but in Britain there was not such a long preamble to the introduction of bronze working. The techniques of making and using bronze already had a long history before they arrived in the British Isles, enabling the prehistoric British population to bypass the copper era very rapidly in favour of bronze.

The skills of the metal workers were probably imported to Britain, without a mass migration or an invasion of other peoples who set about obliterating the natives. The manufacture of metals demanded specialists on a far greater scale than the manufacture of flint or stone implements, most of which could be made at home by people who learned their techniques from their families or communities. The sources of flint, and of the highly valued stone suitable for ceremonial axes, were not necessarily local, but a distribution system was evolved and communities were supplied with the necessary materials or finished objects. The same principles applied to the search for metal ores, but it seems likely that the people who lived near the various sources of ores gained an immediate advantage and strong bargaining power over the people who needed the ore but had no access to sources in their own territory. Then there were the specialist manufacturers who understood the processes of extracting metal from the ore and shaping it, not something that could be done in every home like the manufacture of pottery. Society changed subtly to accommodate these new developments.

There were no doubt powerful individuals in late Neolithic society, who directed activities in their own areas, holding power by means of their dominant personalities or their religious background. It is not possible to speak of priest-kings or dynasties because there is not enough information about the structure of society. The emergence of leaders does seem to be illustrated by the way in which the late Neolithic and early Bronze Age people treated their dead.

Communal burials were out of fashion by the time Stonehenge was being built. Cremations are so common at Stonehenge itself that it has been described as a cremation cemetery, but apart from the remains of bones there is not much else to facilitate the study of the early Stonehenge people. In the late Neolithic and early Bronze Age, burials as opposed to cremations start to appear, with varied grave goods which provide more information about the individuals who were buried and about the kind of society to which they belonged. The mounds in which these individuals were buried are grouped together under the title of round barrows, which comprise a wide variety of types. Archaeologists distinguish between them by their methods of construction, applying names which refer to their shapes, including bell, bowl, disc, saucer, pond, and ring ditch barrows. Of these, the bowl barrows had the longest history, starting in the mid-third millennium BC.

Some of the burials in the round barrows were richly endowed with grave goods. Usually the body was interred in a pit dug into the earth, as opposed to being laid on the ground and surrounded by a screen of wood or stone, and then covered with earth as in earlier Neolithic times. The new fashion may have had something to do with a belief in gods of the underworld, and may be related to the widespread burial of objects in pits in many of the monuments, a long-lived tradition that spanned the Neolithic and early Bronze Age. The principal burial in the round barrows was usually one individual, but secondary burials were made, sometimes of cremated bones, or on occasion the barrow could be enlarged and another burial placed on top of the first one, with an extra mound of earth built over it.

The items buried with the deceased typically include bronze axes, knives and daggers, tools for various crafts, and dress ornaments, sometimes of gold. There is also evidence of leather, bone and wooden objects, and of textiles. It is possible that textiles had been developed in the Neolithic era but no evidence has been found. The first known remnant of cloth was found in a Bronze Age burial. Weapons always signify warrior burials, and craftsmen were buried with their tools. Some burials are of women, with rich dress ornament. It is tempting to view these individuals with weapons and high-quality grave goods as the leaders of society or members of a ruling class, but without further evidence of the structure of society this must remain a theory.

One of the most famous burials in a round barrow in the vicinity of Stonehenge is the one at Boscombe Down near Amesbury. Its principal occupant has been labelled the Amesbury Archer. Examination of the skeleton revealed that he was in his thirties when he died, and at some point in his life he had lost his left kneecap, probably not accidentally but by deliberate mutilation, leaving his leg bone wasted and probably permanently unhealed. The unfortunate man also had a tooth abscess. Dating evidence placed him somewhere in the late third millennium, between 2400 and 2200 BC, so he would have known what Stonehenge looked like and may even have taken part in ceremonies there. The most startling fact, resulting from analysis of his teeth, is that he was not a native Briton but had started life in the region of the Alps. How he came to be buried in the Stonehenge area is not known, but it is suggested that Stonehenge itself was a healing centre of great renown, and the man had travelled there for relief from his suffering, just as people travel to Lourdes nowadays.

The grave goods buried with the man included fifteen arrowheads and two wrist guards, so he was dubbed the Archer from this evidence. If he was buried with his bow, there was no evidence of it. Other items included three copper knives, gold ornaments, and bone objects. Alongside him there were the remains of five children, three of them cremated, and an adolescent and two men. These children and men were not necessarily associated with him, except for one young man who was buried near him, who proved on analysis to be a relative. This individual was not from the Alps, but from southern England. Speculation as to their family history and their deaths near Stonehenge cannot answer all the questions, and the appellation of the Amesbury Archer as the King of Stonehenge does nothing to dispel the notion that burials with a variety of splendid grave goods must somehow signify the leaders of society, and that these people built Stonehenge.

There are over 650 round barrows in the Stonehenge area, grouped together in clusters and therefore designated as cemeteries, but no barrows are sited close to the monument itself, as though there was a taboo on burying people within a certain defined zone all around the stones. Some of the barrows were placed on hills where they would be seen from a distance, but visibility was not a prime concern for all of them, so the factors that governed the positioning of the barrows are not fully understood. Some of the round barrows have been dated to the period when Stonehenge was being built, but by far the majority of them belong to the first half of the second millennium, from *c.* 2000 to 1500 BC. After that time, the construction of round barrows ceased, though secondary burials were sometimes inserted into the mounds.

Beaker pottery, Beaker people? Probably not

According to previous theories, outmoded now, the presence in burials and other archaeological sites of a specific kind of pottery, labelled Beakers after their distinctive shape, was indicative of a group of people who had invaded Britain, bringing their pottery with them. It was thought that they also introduced metal working and all the associated changes in society that these revolutionary new fashions engendered. Given these assumptions, it was probably inevitable that these allegedly new people were also credited with the building of the last phase of Stonehenge.

There seemed to be considerable support for the invasion hypothesis from burials in the long and round barrows. Skull types from these barrows displayed significant differences, those from long barrows belonging to long-headed people, and those from round barrows belonging to round-headed people. This provided a template for racial types as well a useful mnemonic for archaeologists, long heads in long barrows, round heads in round barrows, and round barrows were presumed to have succeeded long barrows. The difference in skull types strongly suggested the presence of two distinct races, so the theory evolved that the so-called Beaker people must have appeared en masse, and the earlier population had either been deliberately obliterated or had simply disappeared because of the strong competition from the invaders for land and resources.

The theory that there was a specific group of people associated with Beaker pottery is now discredited. The dating of the pottery has been revised, removing the close association of the so-called Beaker culture with round barrows and metal working. It is now known that the indigenous population had already been building round barrows for some time before the arrival of Beaker pottery, so it cannot be said that new people introduced new pottery as well as new burial customs. The association with the introduction of metals is also disproved, since metalworking is now known to have predated the arrival of Beaker pottery.

Rather than a wholesale invasion and conquest, there was probably a gradual infiltration of people into Britain, bringing with them Beaker pottery styles. It was probably by peaceful means of trade and exchange that the spread of Beaker pottery was engendered by the new settlers. Beaker pottery is flat-bottomed, the vessels shaped like a beaker with a curved waist, and decorated with incised markings in geometric patterns. It is widespread on the Continent, embracing several modern countries and perhaps different prehistoric racial types. The first examples in Britain may have come from the Netherlands, around 2400 BC and the fashion survived until *c.* 2000 BC. The earliest Beaker pots from British sites are noticeably finer than the later versions. This probably means that the imports were copied locally but the copies were not so expertly done.

With regard to the Stonehenge area, Beakers are found in burials in the outlying areas – for instance, the Amesbury Archer had five Beakers among his grave goods – but there seems to have been an exclusion zone in the immediate vicinity of the stone monument, where burials do not contain the pottery. There may have been some sacred taboo attached to the locale, respected by the inhabitants, or alternatively there may have been actual hostilities between the indigenous population and the newcomers. Possibly around the same time as the Archer was buried with his multiple grave goods, another individual was buried without pomp and ceremony in a pit near the north-east entrance to Stonehenge. Three arrows, shot at close range, had penetrated his ribs, where the arrowheads were still embedded. This burial has all the hallmarks of a murder rather than a dedicatory interment or a sacrifice. The grave was not carefully dug, suggesting a hasty procedure to remove all evidence of the deed. The reasons why the man was killed remain unknown, but together with the fact that Beakers do not seem to have penetrated the Stonehenge area, the death of this man has been associated with antagonism, or at least serious misunderstanding, between the new people and the natives.

The Bronze Age

The establishment of agriculture and the domestication of animals had its roots in the protracted Neolithic era, but only on a semi-sedentary basis, which makes it much more difficult to detect traces of Neolithic farms and fields in the landscape. Towards the end of the Neolithic era, when it merged with the Bronze Age, the first signs emerge of a more settled way of life. For the first time it is possible to speak of farmsteads and field boundaries, on a larger scale than is possible for the Neolithic period, where the evidence is fragmentary, requiring supplementation by conjectural synthesis of several different sites.

The proliferation of round barrows and the decline of the earlier communal long barrows went hand in hand with a comparable declining use of the communal monuments like Stonehenge. This means that as society changed there was no further need for ritual gatherings of wider communities. Social life became more localised, with support networks of local roads and tracks connecting the settlement sites. As the more sedentary way of life developed, the ritual landscapes were gradually forgotten, along with the religious beliefs and practices that had accompanied them.

The clearest evidence for Bronze Age settlement derives from the Dartmoor Reaves, where traces of houses, farms and fields have been preserved. The dwellings and farmlands were abandoned when the climate changed for the worse, and the remains have not been ploughed out on the moors as would have been the case if the farms had been on lower-lying ground. The evidence for Neolithic houses is not abundant, and what has been found is debatable, consisting for the most part of rectangular buildings, outlined by their post holes. The houses of the Bronze Age, as demonstrated on Dartmoor, were uniformly round, a tradition that survived into the Iron Age and the Roman occupation.

The people of the LNEBA who buried their dead with grave goods in round barrows gradually altered their ways of dealing with their dead. There are few if any burials with rich grave goods, so it seems that society became more uniform if not more equal. Inevitably, rich burials are interpreted as an indication of chiefdoms, if only of small groups, so the lack of such burials makes it harder to discern leaders of society. It is likely that people were divided up into smaller units, and concentrated on their livelihoods and their immediate surroundings, without the need for communal ceremonials at the larger monuments. In this context the henge at Durrington Walls went out of use. It is thought that the Stonehenge people lived there in their wooden dwellings, connected to their stone monument for the dead by the River Avon. Whatever their beliefs and customs for their ancestors, new ways of life with different beliefs eventually obliterated them. Ancestor worship and communal ceremonial rites for the dead died out, and so Stonehenge became redundant. The latest pottery found at Durrington Walls belongs to the Beaker period, so around 1800 BC the last people to live there deserted the site and dispersed. This does not preclude a continued use of Stonehenge as a funerary site, or indeed for any other purpose, by the people who remained in the area or came to settle there at a later period.

For some time, people clung to what they knew. Although the manufacture of bronze axes developed quite rapidly, they did not become universal. In parallel with the use of bronze, the technically competent flint knappers made creditable copies of bronze axes, though as time went on the manufacturing techniques of flint implements started to decline, though it did not die out altogether until the Iron Age. The decline may indicate a changing fashion and a reduced demand for flint tools and in particular for flint axes. On a practical basis the cutting edge of a bronze axe is sharper than a stone or flint axe, and less prone to wear and tear. A stone axe can easily shatter and cannot be repaired, whereas if a bronze axe becomes blunt it can be sharpened.

The principal ingredient in the manufacture of bronze is copper, which was sought after and mined by the prehistoric people. A relatively recent discovery is the copper-mining industry at the Great Orme in Llandudno, North Wales. Industrial activity was presumably organised by someone or by a group, rather than being a free-for-all where anyone could come and find copper ore, and there was presumably a distribution mechanism, but this is to enter the realm of conjecture.

There are indications that bronze tools and weapons were accorded respect if not reverence. Neolithic builders used to leave antler picks and shoulder blade shovels in their ditches, possibly as dedicatory offerings, and the bronze implements were treated in the same way. Many archaeological finds seem to have been ritually deposited in the earth or in lakes, rather than just casually thrown away. They may have been dedicated to the earth, or a deity signifying the earth, or to a water deity. Such rituals were perhaps substituted for those that had once been carried out at the large monuments. Water had always been a significant feature in the Neolithic period, when many monuments were connected with or focused on rivers, just as Stonehenge was connected with Durrington Walls, but in the post Stonehenge era the focus on water was accentuated, implying a religious belief system strongly involved with it. Perhaps it survives in the habit of throwing coins into wishing wells and fountains.

8

EVER AFTER, *c.* 700 BC TO MODERN TIMES

After the population of the Stonehenge area settled down on their farmsteads and the full benefit of the so-called Neolithic revolution eventually came to fruition, Stonehenge was abandoned and largely forgotten. For the farmers of the Bronze Age the monument was surplus to requirements. The rituals and beliefs that had sustained the Mesolithic and Neolithic eras faded away, with perhaps a few remnants permeating the new way of life. The emphasis was on smaller communities rather than the larger gatherings that had characterised the societies of the causewayed enclosures and the henge monuments. Tribal society was emerging.

The Iron Age

The Iron Age is the first period when it is possible to speak of tribes and to discern the territorial boundaries between them, though the political organisation of the tribes was rarely stable or permanent. Boundaries fluctuated, smaller tribes were subsumed by larger and more powerful ones, sometimes creating new federations with new names. This can be illustrated at the very beginning of the Roman period. When Julius Caesar invaded Britain in 55 and 54 BC, he provided an account of his exploits as part of his *Gallic War*. He names a small number of tribes which he encountered in southern Britain, but just under a century later, when the Romans invaded and conquered Britain from AD 43 onwards, these tribes are not heard of again. Even during the Roman occupation tribal names changed. In the third century AD, the northern tribes re-emerged with new federations and new names, which Cassius Dio explains in a brief comment that some smaller tribes had been absorbed into the new larger groupings.

For about a thousand years after the abandonment of Stonehenge and Durrington Walls the immediate area was left alone, reverting to grassland. At Stonehenge there is no sign that people of the Iron Age ever used the site or even visited it. This is true of the stone circles all over Britain, suggesting that the Iron Age people scrupulously avoided the older cult centres, perhaps because of superstitious fear and awe, or because they were totally preoccupied with their own affairs, with their own rituals and beliefs, and a primary need for defence, involving fortifications and the establishment of a warrior society.

Possibly the most iconic feature of the Iron Age is the hill fort. These monuments started to emerge around the seventh century BC. Two relatively small ones were built on either side of the River Avon, within reach of Stonehenge but not in close proximity, one at Ogbury and another near Amesbury, called Vespasian's Camp. The early hill forts were generally quite small compared to later ones. The establishment of larger forts suggests that tribes amalgamated under a strong leader, determined to expand his territory at the expense of smaller tribes. This was a constant feature of tribal life that led eventually to displaced leaders appealing to the Romans for reinstatement and assistance. The last chief to do so arrived at the court of the Emperor Claudius, providing an excuse for invasion, conquest and occupation that lasted for nearly four centuries.

Romans

Although the Romans knew of Britain long before they converted it into a province, and contact was maintained even after the withdrawal in the fifth century AD, not one author, writing in Latin or Greek, mentions Stonehenge. It is feasible that some accounts were made of it, perhaps for official reports, and it is also possible that before the Roman conquest the more intrepid explorers or traders saw or heard of the monument, but no record of it has survived. One ancient author, Diodorus Siculus (the Sicilian), gave an account of a circular temple, without precisely locating it. His work is third-hand, derived from Hecataeus of Abdera, who made extracts from the account given by the Greek explorer Pytheas of Marseilles. The work of these two authors has been lost, but survives in fragments copied or quoted by later authors, of whom Diodorus Siculus, writing in the first century BC, is one.

During the fourth century BC Pytheas had made a voyage around Britain, but it is not certain what he actually saw. According to Hecataeus, as reported by Diodorus, Pytheas described an island, about the same size as Sicily, in the seas beyond the land of the Celts. The inhabitants were called the Hyperboreans, who worshipped Apollo. A circular temple dedicated to this god was known to the Greeks, some of whom who had visited it, and left offerings and inscriptions with Greek lettering there. Hecataeus goes on to say that from the island the moon appears to be very close to the earth, and the features of its surface can be clearly seen. Every nineteen years, when the stars return to the same places in the heavens, the god visits the temple and dances all night long from the vernal equinox to the rising of the Pleiades. This nineteen-year cycle is presumably associated with the 18.6-year cycle of the moon.

At first sight the mention of a circular temple, even though it is not stated that it is made of standing stones, together with hints of worship of the sun god Apollo and of the moon, evokes a picture of Stonehenge, but that is because it is the most famous prehistoric circular temple known at the present time. As Aubrey Burl points out, the closeness of the moon to the earth and the association with the vernal equinox and the Pleiades is not a configuration that can be applied to Stonehenge, but all three criteria can be satisfied at the stone circle at Callanish on the Isle of Lewis. On his voyage around Britain, Pytheas may have seen the stone circle, or heard of it from the natives.

Whatever he saw and described, though remarkable enough in itself, it was not Stonehenge. Even if it had been Stonehenge, it would be questionable whether the ceremonials carried out in the fourth century BC bore any relation to the practices of the Neolithic and Bronze Age builders of Stonehenge thousands of years earlier.

The major Greek and Roman works dealing with Britain, such as Caesar's brief account of his battles, Suetonius's *Geography*, or Tacitus's *Histories* and *Annals*, are devoid of any reference to Stonehenge or any other stone circle. Tacitus also wrote a biography of his father-in-law Gnaeus Julius Agricola, who was successively military tribune legionary legate and governor in Britain, but although this work would have given Tacitus the opportunity to describe British monuments more fully, there is no hint of stone circles. These monuments had presumably not escaped the attention of the Romans, but the fact that no one considered it worth the effort of describing them implies that they were of no interest to the governors or the armies. If these sites had been used by the natives as gathering places for ceremonials, or more pertinently for the purpose of fomenting tribal revolt, somewhere there ought to be a mention in one of the works of the ancient authors. The Romans usually designated places where the natives could legally hold meetings under military supervision, and though not all the place names or sites are known, the lack of any reference to a stone circle implies that the monuments of their ancestors were ignored by the population of Roman Britain. This is supported by the lack of any Iron Age finds at stone circles in general and at Stonehenge in particular.

The Romans did not settle within the immediate confines of Stonehenge, but villas were established in the wider area around it. The land was farmed, and though it was not one of the most prosperous areas of Roman Britain, nor was it among the poorest. The Romano-Britons clearly visited the site, as attested by the stray finds at Stonehenge, but perhaps they were just tourists, full of curiosity about the stones, but not even considering enacting any rituals or ceremonies there. Some Romans may have been responsible for removal of one or two stones, but this cannot be proved. A recent suggestion, made after the discovery of Roman coins and pottery at Stonehenge, is that the Romans did not ignore or neglect the monument, but actively tried to repair it. Such activity would not necessarily find its way into recorded history.

Anglo-Saxons

The first Saxons arrived in Britain some considerable time before the Romans abandoned the province in the early fifth century. Saxons were recruited into the army as auxiliary soldiers, living side by side with the Romano-British population. To the Romans, the name 'Saxon' perhaps did not refer to an individual race, but was used in much the same way as tribesmen from the Danube area and eastern Europe, regardless of origin, were all classified under the non-specific label 'Scythians'. The finds that are associated with the arrival of the Saxons in Britain have been labelled as Germanic, but the racial origin of the finds is now disputed, since it is clear that the Roman army of the late fourth and early fifth centuries was issued with military equipment of Germanic type, so the finds do not necessarily indicate an influx of Saxons. However, it is not in doubt that the Romans recruited Saxon tribesmen to swell the ranks of the army. The Saxons of the early fifth century did not shun Roman sites, but settled near the towns. It was only much later that the towns and villas of the former province were avoided and left to decay.

Close to Stonehenge, some Saxons settled at Amesbury. They knew about the monument in the vicinity, bestowing on it the name by which it is known today, derived from the Saxon *Stan Hengcen*, meaning the hanging stones. As already mentioned, this term could simply refer to the construction, where the lintels appear to hang in the air above the uprights. But the discovery of the grave of a young man, buried just outside the Sarsen Circle, suggests that the term hanging stones had another more sinister meaning. The grave was dug at some time in the seventh century, and it was not a reverential burial of someone who had died of disease or as the result of an accident. The man had been decapitated. He was from the local area, according to an examination of his teeth, so he was not a visiting foreigner who had broken some taboo and been killed for his pains. Either this was a murder, hastily covered up, or an execution. The presence of two post holes, one on either side of his grave, has been interpreted as the foundation for a wooden gallows. For the Saxons, Stonehenge may have been a place of death just as it was in the Neolithic era, but not for burials of cremated bones of the local populace. It was probably a place of summary justice.

Whatever Stonehenge meant to the Saxons, there is no surviving literary reference to it. No Anglo-Saxon poems mention it, and the earliest historians, Gildas, Nennius, and the Venerable Bede, all ignore it. Proper appreciation of the monument was left to the Normans.

Normans

About four or five decades after the Norman Conquest, a monk called Henry of Huntingdon, who lived from 1084 to 1155, wrote a history of England, or more precisely a history of the English, *Historia Anglorum*, which was produced *c.* 1129. He listed Stonehenge as the second wonder of Britain. He may not have visited the site, but he knew that it was fashioned from very large stones, which he describes as columns with stones across their tops, like great doorways. He also mentioned that no one knew how the stones had been raised, or what purpose they served. The Normans were prolific builders, and the point about raising the stones could imply that someone among the Norman ruling class, or at least someone who knew how to build things from stone, had looked at the monument and pondered. Henry of Huntingdon's description is the earliest recorded reference to Stonehenge. It is also more than just a casual mention. It is an acknowledgement of the astonishing labours that produced the monument, and of the fact that it is an almost miraculous construction provoking wonder, awe and large amounts of speculation.

The most tantalising literary reference to Stonehenge has already been mentioned in connection with the transport of the Bluestones. Geoffrey of Monmouth's *History of the Kings of Britain* (*Historia Regum Britanniae*) engenders confusion rather than elucidation, because although he resorts to a magical explanation of how the stones arrived at Stonehenge from Ireland, he seems to some modern authors to preserve a tradition that the stones came from the west. The Bluestones came from south-west Wales, so the connection was made. The fact that Geoffrey specifically mentioned neither Bluestones nor Wales is explained away as the embellishment over many centuries of the original tradition. The modern dichotomy over the transport of the stones by human or glacial action would have arisen without the contribution of Geoffrey of Monmouth. He simply adds a further complication to the various theories.

Medieval chroniclers

Geoffrey's work was immensely popular for many years. His story of how Merlin brought the stones from Ireland was taken up in later works. From the end of the twelfth century to the beginning of the fifteenth century, the tale was presented as fact. In the fourteenth century an illustration was produced showing Merlin placing one of the lintels on top of two uprights, with an appreciative audience gazing with wonder at his achievement. Then in the middle of the fifteenth century, doubts began to set in. In 1458, William Caxton, the first English printer, published *The Chronicle of England*, written by an unknown author. In this book, the exploits of Merlin at Stonehenge are presented as a fabulous tale.

The antiquarians

From the sixteenth century onwards, various antiquarians began to take a more serious interest in Stonehenge. Until the nineteenth century the learned men who examined prehistoric monuments were strongly influenced by what they knew of the architecture of Greece and Rome, much of it still visible, and the works of the ancient authors. The extant literature concerning Britain began with Julius Caesar's account of his brief invasions in the first century BC, and continued with Strabo's *Geography*, Tacitus's *Histories* and *Annals*, and the various statements to be found in the works of Pliny. All these authors worked in the first century AD. It was natural that the antiquarians should refer to classical architecture and literature to interpret what they saw at Stonehenge and other prehistoric monuments. There were no scientific dating techniques available to them, so none of them can be blamed for failing to establish exactly how extremely old stone circles and henges were. The nearest estimate of the vast age of Stonehenge was given in the early eighteenth century by Edmond Halley, who accompanied William Stukeley on one of his surveys. Halley examined the stones very closely, and concluded from the amount of weathering that he detected on their surfaces that they must have been standing for at least 3,000 years. Perhaps this estimate seemed far too preposterous for anyone to take it seriously, originating as it did from an astronomer and mathematician who was not otherwise noted for his antiquarian pursuits. Stukeley noted the observations, but made no use of them in his work on Stonehenge.

In Tudor times, and possibly even earlier, various people had dug into the barrows and Stonehenge itself, not in a spirit of enquiry but as treasure seekers. By this time Stonehenge had begun to show signs of decay. Long ago, possibly even in prehistoric times, the stones of one of the Trilithons had suffered, Stone 55 and the lintel 156 having fallen down, and as a result of the fall the second upright, Stone 56, had been dragged forwards and remained in this tilted position, the angle increasing steadily as time went on. A drawing produced in the 1570s shows this clearly but also reveals that the Slaughter Stone and its partner were still upright at the north-east entrance.

Inigo Jones

The first serious study of Stonehenge was made by the architect Inigo Jones, after he had visited the site with James I in 1620. Jones had already been made Surveyor of the King's Works in 1615, so he was the logical candidate to make a survey of the ancient monument. He camped out near Stonehenge to do so.

Having been to Italy and seen great Roman buildings for himself, Jones was influenced by ancient building techniques. In particular he referred to the *Ten Books of Architecture* by the Roman architect Vitruvius. A manuscript of this work was copied by monks in the ninth century, but not rediscovered until 1414. It became a widely known and respected manual, and since it was the most ancient text on building, and the true antiquity of Stonehenge was not known, Jones thought that the Romans were responsible for building it.

Looking at the Trilithons (not to be so labelled until Stukeley coined the term in the eighteenth century), Jones thought that originally there must have been an enclosed circle, and accordingly his reconstruction drawing shows a circular arrangement of six Trilithons, even though the monument as visible in his day lacked comparable stones at the open north-east side. He discovered that nothing had been built in the ground between the stone circles and the bank and ditch, but on examining the surrounding earthwork he thought that there had been three entrances. The north-eastern one was unmistakable, and framing the entrance there were standing stones, formed by the Slaughter Stone and its companion inside the bank and the Heel Stone outside it, which arrangement begged for a fourth stone next to the Heel Stone to complete the pattern of four stones. Jones took this to have been the format for his two other proposed entrances, one in the north-west, and one in the south, which would have formed a triangle, with each gateway framed by four standing stones. His monumental entrances had never existed, but Jones cannot be taken to task for the mistake. Without modern equipment and techniques, or any knowledge of prehistory, any archaeologist may have come up with the same theory.

Around the same time as Jones's survey, some excavations, or rather trial diggings, were carried out on the orders of the Duke of Buckingham, close friend of James I. This enterprise was conducted in pursuit of treasure rather than knowledge, and if there were any spectacular finds it is not known what happened to them. But the work did reveal that burials had been made inside and outside the bank and ditch. Jones interpreted them as sacrifices made in the temple.

Jones left notes and drawings which he never published as a full report. He died in 1652, and three years later his nephew by marriage, John Webb, produced a book from Jones's work, called *The Most Notable Antiquity of Great Britain, vulgarly called Stone-heng*.

John Aubrey

Shortly before the death of Inigo Jones, the future king Charles II visited Stonehenge in October 1651. He was a fugitive after the Battle of Worcester, so he cannot have afforded a great deal of time to examine the monument, but it left a lasting impression on him. After the Restoration, Charles was interested to learn that John Aubrey considered the stone circle at Avebury to be a much more impressive monument than Stonehenge. In 1663 the King and his entourage and John Aubrey visited Avebury, and the King climbed Silbury Hill nearby. Three years later he asked Aubrey to survey Stonehenge. Aubrey had known the monument since childhood. He was a serious scholar with a perceptive mind and a no-nonsense attitude to the various myths that had grown up around Stonehenge. He dismissed the idea that Merlin had brought the Sarsen Stones from Ireland, because he knew that they had come from the Marlborough Downs, where some of them can still be seen lying on the ground.

Inigo Jones had suggested that Stonehenge was a Roman structure, and in 1663, the same year that Charles and Aubrey visited Avebury, a book was published drawing attention to similar stone circles in Denmark, concluding that it was the Danes who built Stonehenge. Aubrey discounted both these suggestions, because he knew that there were other stone circles in northern Scotland and Ireland, where the Romans had not established a permanent presence, and also in Wales where the influence of the Danes had not penetrated. Therefore it followed that Stonehenge was already standing on Salisbury Plain when the Romans arrived in Britain in the first century AD.

When Aubrey conducted his survey, some of the Sarsen Stones on the east had fallen down. His plan shows that the three standing stones at the north-east entrance were still upright, and Aubrey deduced that the Heel Stone was one of a series of stones lining an Avenue, just as he had seen at Avebury, where the West Kennet Avenue is still marked by lines of stones on each side. Accordingly he tentatively drew in the lines of the proposed Avenue leading from the north-east entrance of Stonehenge. Several decades later, William Stukeley would discover the traces of the Avenue, thus proving that Aubrey's assumption was correct, without perhaps knowing that the earlier scholar had already suggested it.

The most famous contribution that Aubrey made to the study of Stonehenge was his discovery of a few depressions around the inside of the encircling bank, which he thought represented holes which once held stones. These were rediscovered in the twentieth century, a total of fifty-six more or less regularly spaced holes, labelled Aubrey Holes after their first discoverer.

Convinced that the stone circle at Stonehenge predated the Roman invasion, Aubrey looked around for the most likely builders. It was clearly a religious or ritual site, so he hinted that it must have been the Druids who built it, the most famous priestly caste who inhabited the island in the centuries before the Romans, and described by Caesar in Gaul, and by Tacitus when the Roman governor Suetonius Paullinus attacked them in their stronghold of Anglesey. Aubrey did not specifically or emphatically assign the monument to the Druids. That was left to William Stukeley.

William Stukeley

Stukeley was the man who contributed the most to the study of Stonehenge in the early eighteenth century. It is possibly fair to say that he was obsessed by the monument rather than having merely a strong interest in it, but his obsession led to new discoveries and a more rounded appreciation of the landscape around Stonehenge.

From 1721 to 1724 Stukeley worked in and around Stonehenge. He coined the term Trilithons for the tall stones of the Horseshoe, and investigated the recumbent Altar Stone, where he found that the chalk around it was tightly compacted and could not have been disturbed by digging a socket, therefore the Altar Stone had never been placed upright in its location in the curve of the Horseshoe. He confirmed Aubrey's suggestion that there was an Avenue leading out of the north-east entrance, and he supposed like Aubrey that there were stones lining the Avenue inside the two banks, but although he found holes where the postulated stones had once stood, he did not include them on his published plan. North of Stonehenge he discerned the Cursus, so named because he thought it was a racetrack like the Roman circuses. He investigated the barrows surrounding Stonehenge, classifying them into groups based on their sizes, attributing the larger ones to the burials of the most important priests and the successively smaller ones to successively less exalted individuals. He could not have known that they were not all contemporary. He would have been astonished at the centuries that divided them, and probably incredulous at the great antiquity of the earliest ones.

Stukeley's conclusions on Stonehenge were published in 1740, as *Stonehenge, a temple restor'd to the British Druids*. Three years later he also published a book on Avebury, also attributing this stone circle to the Druids. The association of Stonehenge and Druids is now so indelibly imprinted on modern minds that it will probably never be eradicated, but lacking any means of dating Stonehenge more accurately, Stukeley ought not to be censured for his claims. As a tribute to his energy, enthusiasm, accuracy and acute observational abilities, it is possibly true to say that if he could have been presented with the information now available to scholars, that Stonehenge preceded the Druids by thousands of years, Stukeley would have possessed sufficient integrity in his search for truth to have abandoned his Druidical obsessions, and would have taken up Neolithic ones instead.

The nineteenth century

After Stukeley, there was a dearth of enthusiastic scholars who produced work on Stonehenge. Perhaps Stukeley's work embodied the last word on the monument. In 1747 a survey and plan of the stone circles was produced by John Wood. The accuracy of the plan was confirmed by Flinders Petrie in the 1870s. Meanwhile Stonehenge was suffering from decay and lack of attention. Trilithons 57 and 58, and their lintel, fell down in January 1797.

At the beginning of the nineteenth century, Sir Richard Colt Hoare and William Cunnington started to investigate some of the barrows in the Stonehenge area. Archaeology was in its infancy, and still had a long way to go, as investigators learned empirically how to study and record what they found, but Hoare produced reports that approached the sort of recording that would be required nowadays.

In 1802, Hoare investigated the Altar Stone, and in 1810 he turned his attention to the Slaughter Stone, where he discovered that the base was rougher than the body of the stone, concluding that the stone had once been upright in its socket. This stone was shown as a standing stone on Aubrey's plan but it was not until the twentieth century that his work was recognised and given proper attention.

Looking at the Sarsen Stones and the Bluestones, Hoare realised that they were geologically quite different. Like Aubrey, he knew that the Sarsens came from the Marlborough Downs, but he did not know where the Bluestones originated, except that he was quite certain that they had nothing to do with Merlin or Ireland.

Flinders Petrie

Petrie had already studied the antiquities of Egypt before he came to Stonehenge to carry out meticulous measurements in 1877. He thought that standard units of measurement could be applied to the monument, just as he had been able to demonstrate for the pyramids of Egypt. What he found convinced him that the builders of Stonehenge had used a mixture of prehistoric, Phoenician and also Roman units in the construction. This was before the great antiquity of all the elements of Stonehenge had been established, but his assertion that Roman units had been used only served, for a while, to complicate the dating of the monument.

A more lasting contribution to the study of Stonehenge was Petrie's numbering system for all the stones, a task which involved sorting out from the jumble of upright and fallen stones exactly what had belonged to which set up. By Petrie's day Stonehenge was desperately in need of some tender loving care, more of the stones having fallen down since the first surveys by Inigo Jones and John Aubrey. Having surveyed and measured all parts of Stonehenge, Petrie identified individual elements and numbered them accordingly, starting from the right-hand or eastern side of the north-eastern entrance and moving clockwise around the circle. He allocated a single number to broken stones, distinguishing the individual pieces by adding a letter to the number. Where there were gaps in the circles, Petrie estimated from the spacing of the extant stones where the hypothetical missing ones might have been and gave them all numbers, though it should be pointed out that not all scholars agree that the circles were ever completed. Petrie started by numbering the Sarsen Circle (1 to 30), then the Bluestone Circle (31 to 49), then the Trilithon Horseshoe (51 to 60), the Bluestone Horseshoe (61 to 72). He grouped together the outlier stones, with the Four Station Stones numbered consecutively in the customary clockwise direction. All the lintels, whether they were still in place or on the ground, were allocated numbers according to their higher numbered uprights, with one hundred added, so that for instance the lintel of Trilithon 57 and 58 became 158. This was a brilliant common-sense approach that brought clarity to the existing remains, and it has not been radically altered. Discoveries that were made long after Petrie's survey, such as the Aubrey Holes, the Q and R holes, and the Y and Z holes, are all numbered according to his clockwise scheme.

The twentieth century

Although Stonehenge was still privately owned at the beginning of the twentieth century, it had always been a major attraction for visitors, and access to the site had been allowed. But by the beginning of the twentieth century it was beginning to decay so badly that it was dangerous. Sarsen Stone 22 and its lintel fell in 1899. Other stones in danger of falling had been unceremoniously propped up with railway sleepers. The owner, Sir Edmond Antrobus, accordingly restricted access to the site. Something would have to be done if Stonehenge was to be prevented from collapsing altogether, and the first action to be taken was to raise the dangerously leaning Trilithon 56 and restore it to its original upright position. Sir Edmond offered to pay for the task. This was the first of a series of repairs using modern equipment and modern methods to produce the version of Stonehenge that is known today. Trilithon 56 is now anachronistically embedded in concrete to secure it, concrete not having been invented until Roman times, long after the prehistoric builders tried to secure their standing stones.

Excavations of Stonehenge began in earnest after the First World War. After the death of Sir Edmond Antrobus, the site was bought by Cecil Chubb, who gave it to the nation in 1918. William Hawley (another William, almost a prerequisite first name for any study of Stonehenge) started to excavate the eastern half of Stonehenge in 1919. In the 1920s he discovered the Aubrey Holes, the Y and Z holes, the post holes across the north-eastern entrance, and those at the southern sector.

A programme of repairs was started. In total, in the years between Hawley's first excavations in 1919 and the last repair in 1964, Sarsen Stones 1, 2, 4, 5, 7, 19, 20, 22, 29 and 30 were replaced in their sockets, and where necessary some of them were set in concrete. The Bluestones of the circle, Stones 41, 42, 43 and 45, received attention, as did Stones 60, 69 and 70 in the Bluestone Horseshoe. The major achievement, in 1958 and 1959, was the re-erection of Trilithon 57 and 58, complete with lintel 158. A catalogue of all the repairs carried out in the first half of the twentieth century demonstrates the vastly different appearance of Stonehenge before the creation of the version that is visible today. It has justifiably been designated a World Heritage Site, for which a management plan was drawn up in 2000, revised in 2009. Various controversies are still ongoing, not the least of which is the disruptive presence of the A303, along which the traffic roars by or sometimes gridlocks itself, too close to the monument for comfort.

Astronomical alignments and standard measurements?

Influenced perhaps by the orientation of the pyramids of Egypt, some authors have proposed that various significant stars can be observed from Stonehenge, and that the prehistoric builders

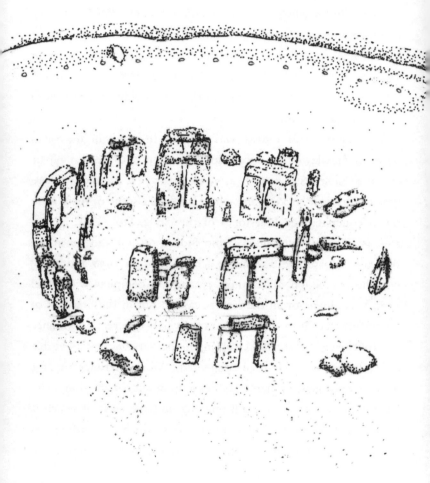

Fig. 17. This drawing shows the extant state of Stonehenge after an ongoing series of repairs in the twentieth century, up to the mid 1960s. Some stones were completely re-erected, others pulled upright from their leaning positions. Some fallen lintels were replaced. The monument seen today may still seem a little confusing, but thanks to all the work carried out on it, Stonehenge is much tidier and more comprehensible to modern visitors than it was to archaeologists of the nineteenth and early twentieth centuries. Drawn by Jacqui Taylor.

deliberately arranged the stones to enable their priests or shamans to watch the risings and settings of certain astronomical features. This may be a correct assumption, but it must be acknowledged that observers who watch the heavens from a circular monument on a flat plain, with an unrestricted view of the horizons, cannot fail to notice certain stars, even if this had not been the primary purpose of erecting the monument. Many of the proposed alignments may not be in question, but the unknown factors are the intentions of the Neolithic and Bronze Age builders. Their astronomical knowledge may have been quite profound, but it is perhaps more likely that their main focus was on the most visible and most powerful influences on the earth, namely the behaviour of the sun and the moon.

It was William Stukeley who first noted the alignment of Stonehenge with the midsummer sunrise through the north-east entrance. He may not have been the first to make the connection but he was the first to describe it in print. He was fully aware that the Heel Stone did not mark the event. He described how the sun, observed from the centre of the monument, actually rose to the left of the stone.

The association with the sun was generally accepted in the nineteenth century. As described in a previous chapter, when the Avenue was built the alignment of Stonehenge was changed slightly, enabling even more accurate observations to be made of the sunrise in the north-east in midsummer, and also the sunset in midwinter in the south-west. At Stonehenge, the midsummer risings and settings of the sun cross at right angles, but in other areas and at other latitudes they do not.

When attention began to be focused on the astronomical alignments at Stonehenge, two problems affected the precision

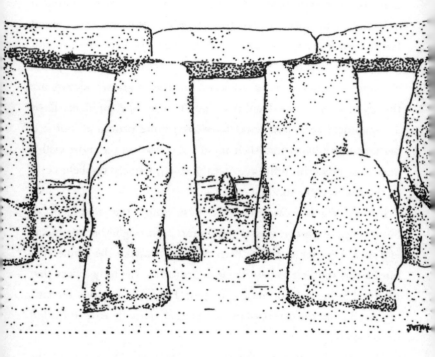

Fig. 18. The classic view of the Heel Stone from inside the monument, framed by the shorter Bluestones and the Sarsen uprights. At the risk of monotonous repetition (see text) the sun does not rise directly over the Heel Stone on midsummer's day, but to its left, a feature which was noted by William Stukeley in the eighteenth century. There were once two upright stones which flanked the rising sun, but only the Heel Stone survives. Photos of the sunrise can be adjusted, weather permitting, so that the sun's disc seems to sit on the top of the Heel Stone. This may not be authentic but it is nonetheless highly atmospheric. Drawn by Jacqui Taylor.

of the calculations. It became vitally important to establish which phases of the monument were contemporary and which were successive, because any measurements made by using all the features of the stone circles at the same time, sometimes using outlying lumps and bumps as well, was bound to skew the results. No prehistoric observer could have used all the features at the same time to match up with various lunar, solar, or stellar alignments. An important facet of sunrises and sunsets is the gradual progression along the horizon as the centuries go by. This is a process known as the obliquity of the ecliptic. Thousands of years ago the sun would have risen even further north than it does now, and therefore even further to the left of the Heel Stone. The point where the sun rises gradually moves to the right, as seen from the centre of Stonehenge. Thousands of years into the future, the sun will eventually rise over the Heel Stone. Since astronomers can calculate where the sun would be rising in 4000 BC, 3000 BC, 2000 BC and so on, it seemed that it ought to be possible to work out the age of Stonehenge by minutely examining the alignment. Up to a point this may be true but an unknown factor influences the conclusions. How, exactly, did the prehistoric builders pinpoint the sunrise?

The rising of the sun is a visibly mobile event, from the first glimmer of light above the horizon to the emergence of the full disc above the horizon. By the time the sun is fully visible it has moved some distance along the horizon, some degrees further away from the place where the light first appeared. Did the prehistoric observers interpret sunrise as the first light of dawn, the rim of the sun when it first showed itself, the left, centre or right of the half disc, or did they wait until the whole disc appeared above the earth, and pinpoint its centre? Lack of knowledge about how the prehistoric builders of Stonehenge observed the sunrise makes it impossible to calculate with any precision the timescale to which the phases of the monument belong.

In addition to the sunrises and sunsets, the Stonehenge people may have been interested in the equinoxes, thought there is no evidence for this assumption. At the equinoxes the days and nights are approximately equal in length. In the spring, around 21 March, and again in the autumn around 23 September, the sun rises almost exactly in the east and sets almost exactly in the west. This could have been observed at Stonehenge. According to an amateur astronomer called Peter Newham, the equinox could be measured by lining up Station Stone 94 in the north-west with a hole near the Heel Stone. The equinoctial alignments at Stonehenge have not been accorded the same prominence as the sunrises.

The Four Station Stones, set in the bank around the stone monument and forming an almost perfect rectangle, are aligned with the midsummer sunrise on their short sides. Peter Newham also discovered that their long sides point to the northernmost moonset. There may have been other uses for the Station Stones, as suggested by Sir Norman Lockyer, who linked them with festivals that are well known in the Iron Age, but which could well have had antecedents in the remote prehistoric past. He suggested that from the centre of Stonehenge, an observer looking towards Stone 93 would be able to observe the sunset in early May, when the Celtic festival of Beltane was held. Similarly, over Stone 91 they could observe the sunrise in early November, when the Iron Age people celebrated Samain.

Aubrey Burl refined the argument to embrace all four of the annual Iron Age festivals in February (Imbolc), May (Beltane), August (Lughnasa) and November (Samain). He suggested that

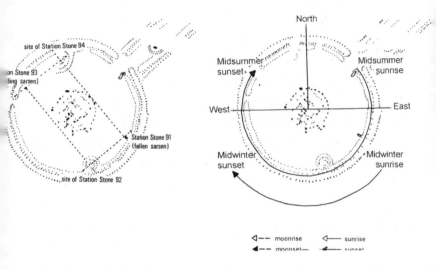

Fig. 19. Diagrams showing the rectangle formed by the Four Station Stones, numbered 91 to 94 following Flinders Petrie's system. The longer sides are oriented to the midsummer sunrise, the shorter ones to the major northern setting of the moon. Sir Norman Lockyer suggested that there may be a connection with two of the four main festivals of the Iron Age that took place in February, May, August and November. Lockyer suggested that from the centre of the circle, looking towards Stone 93 observers would see the sun going down in May, and over Stone 91 they would see the sun rising in November. This theory was revised and augmented by Aubrey Burl to include all four festivals, by using the diagonals across the Station Stones instead of sighting the celestial events from the centre of the circle. In February, the festival of Imbolc would be marked by the sunset as seen from Stone 91 looking towards Stone 93, in May, the setting sun would mark Beltane, looking from Stone 92 to Stone 94, in August sighting from Stone 93 to Stone 91 the sunrise would mark the festival of Lughnasa, and in November Samain would be marked by the sunrise from Stone 94 to 92. The alignments are not entirely accurate, being some degrees short of the exact location according to modern dating of these festivals but an approximation was probably all that was required to start proceedings. Drawn by Jacqui Taylor after Burl 2007 and Darvill 2007.

observers would not place themselves in the centre of Stonehenge, but observations would be made diagonally across the rectangle from the corners. If used in this way, by looking from Stone 92 in the south-east to Stone 94 in the north-west, the May sunset at Beltane could be seen, and the other way from Stone 94 to Stone 92 would point to sunrise at the February festival of Imbolc. The other diagonal, between Stone 91 to 93, pointed to the sunset in August at Lughnasa, and the sunrise in November at Samain. These alignments are not astronomically precise, but it is argued that an approximation would suffice, and it is a fascinating concept that the festivals of the Iron Age may have been celebrated hundreds if not thousands of years earlier, even if it is not known what language the prehistoric participants spoke, or what they called their festivals.

The builders of Stonehenge clearly used some method or methods of measurement in planning the layout of the various elements of the monument, but no one knows precisely how measurements were made. Attempts have been made to translate hypothetical units of length into modern equivalents of feet and inches or metres and centimetres. One problem with this approach is that over the many centuries of its development there may have been several different standard units in use, making it impossible to apply any single standard to the entire structure.

One possible method by which prehistoric people could have measured the projected layout of the circular bank and ditch, and the successive stone circles, is the use of a measuring rod, so that the diameters of circles could have been measured in multiples of the standard rod, and the finer tuning in the spacing of the stones could have been in single units or in subdivisions of it. The existence of such a hypothetical tool is supported by a hazelwood rod found in a grave of the middle Bronze Age in Denmark. This has been interpreted as a standard unit of measurement.

The dimensions of the rod could have been obtained from the human body. In medieval times, cloth was measured in units called 'ells', measured from the hand to the tip of the chin, which was turned away from the outstretched arm. The ancient cubit used in Egypt and mentioned in the Bible was traditionally measured from the elbow to the tip of the middle finger. These units would show some variation from person to person, but any potential variation would not matter if the same measurement was used in the planning stages and the construction of individual monuments.

William Stukeley was one of the first to propose standard measurements for Stonehenge, and he spent many enthusiastic hours on the site trying to work out what that standard might have been. He eventually labelled his hypothetical unit a Druid's cubit, 20.8 inches or 52.8 cm, slightly shorter than the Egyptian cubit. He found that he could not successfully apply his Roman foot of 11.5 inches to any of the parts of Stonehenge, and concluded from this that the Romans had not had anything to do with its construction.

Flinders Petrie, on the other hand, found that his version of the Roman foot, at 11.68 inches could be applied at several places, in multiples of 40, 50, 80 and 100, temporarily confusing the issues of the date of the building and who was responsible for it.

The most important argument for standard units of measurement, not just for Stonehenge, but for megalithic monuments as a whole, originated with Alexander Thom, in the course of his surveys of many monuments in search of astronomical alignments. In the 1950s he proposed a Megalithic Yard of 2.72 feet or 0.829 metres, and a Megalithic Rod of 6.8 feet or 2.07 metres. These measurements could be found in many stone circles, no matter what their shape was. Not all stone circles are truly circular; some are flattened circles, ellipses or even egg-shaped. Nowadays, Thom's Megalithic Yard is not generally accepted, though his work ought to excite admiration for the effort and energy he put into it, visiting and measuring so many prehistoric sites.

At Stonehenge neither the Megalithic Yard nor any of the other standard units that have been proposed can be made to fit all the features of the successive phases. It is more likely that units of measurement applied to small local areas, rather than right across the country for all prehistoric peoples. These units would probably vary as the centuries progressed, each set of builders using their own standards for the successive versions of Stonehenge. They may also have appreciated the humour in the phrase 'How long is a piece of string?'

GLOSSARY

Ard: plough used in the Neolithic period, made of wood with a point hardened by fire, or sometimes a sharp stone was set into the wood to cut the furrows. The plough would be drawn by humans or by animals, and usually the field would be ploughed in criss-cross fashion to ensure that the soil was sufficiently broken up. The ard had no mould board.

Atkinson, R. J. C: archaeologist, professor at the University of Cardiff, who investigated Stonehenge intensively, and whose work is still acknowledged in modern books. He worked in the 1950s and 1960s, producing his book *Stonehenge* in 1956, a work which was revised in 1979. His proposed chronology for Stonehenge, dividing its history into three phases, has since been reconsidered with regard to the dates of a few of the features of the monument, but remains broadly as he first categorised the component parts.

Aubrey, John (1626–1697): antiquarian and historian who investigated several ancient monuments, leaving notes and drawings which were to be produced as a book called *Monumenta Britannica*, but he died before it was published. His work was lodged in the British Museum, and his book was finally produced in the 1980s. He surveyed and drew a plan of Avebury, but when he climbed Silbury Hill with Charles II he could see from this viewpoint that his plan was not correct. He carried out a survey of Stonehenge in 1666 on behalf of the King, in the course of which he discovered some depressions near the bank of earth surrounding the monument. Subsequent antiquarians paid little heed to his discoveries but investigations in the twentieth century vindicated him. A total of fifty-six holes were revealed, arranged in an almost perfect circle. These holes were labelled Aubrey Holes in his honour. Aubrey was responsible for the first association of Stonehenge with the Druids, a theory which was taken up and endorsed by William Stukeley about a century later, and is now ineradicably embedded in modern mythology. John Aubrey was also the author of the entertaining *Brief Lives*, which contains succinct and witty portrayals of his predecessors and contemporaries.

Avebury: henge monument north-west of Stonehenge. The largest of all British henges, Avebury is surrounded by a very deep ditch set inside a bank of earth, enclosing nearly 29 acres. A circle of undressed Sarsen Stones was set up around the perimeter near the inner edge of the ditch, and two smaller stone circles were created in the interior. The northern ring contains the feature known as the Cove, three huge rectangular stones forming three sides of a square, with its opening to the north. The southern circle has a standing stone in the centre, called the Obelisk. These two stone circles are very large, and Stonehenge could easily fit inside them. There are various outlying stones, which may or may not be sight-lines for astronomical purposes, and there may have been earlier phases before the bank and ditch or the two inner circles. The site was purchased, excavated and preserved by Alexander Keiller, whose family fortune derived from the manufacture of marmalade. He had already bought the causewayed enclosure of Windmill Hill nearby.

Avenue: at Stonehenge this refers to the long passageway running north-east from the main entrance, then curving round to the east and south to meet the River Avon. A broad corridor or processional way is flanked by two parallel banks of earth with a ditch on the outer sides. Avenues are known at other henges and stone circles, notably the Kennet Avenue at Avebury, marked on either side by a series of large stones and running for one and a half miles to the Sanctuary, a stone circle which may have been preceded by a circle of wooden posts.

Axe: flint axes were shaped and used in the Mesolithic period, paralleled but not superseded in the Neolithic era by stone axes. Many of these were used for daily activities such as clearing trees and for carpentry, but some finely polished axes were prestige goods, transported for long distances, from the factories such as those in the Lake District and Wales, and occasionally from the Alps. They may have been given as gifts or exchange goods. Metal axes started to appear in the Bronze Age, perhaps as early as the middle of the third millennium BC.

Barrow: (i) Long barrows were Neolithic burial mounds, very large and very long, made of earth covering a series of burial chambers defined by wooden partitions or by large stones. Burials were communal, and not usually carried out until the corpse had been de-fleshed. Bones were often jumbled up together, and usually only some of the long bones and skulls were buried, so complete skeletons are rarely found. Long barrows were trapezoidal in shape, tapering down from the high entrance with two projecting mounds flanking a so-called forecourt, where ceremonials may have been carried out.

(ii) Round barrows overlapped with long barrows and gradually superseded them. Archaeologists have distinguished several different types of round barrow, labelled according to their shapes, such as saucer, bowl, and disc barrows. Bowl barrows were used long before the other types and had the longest history of all round barrows. Communal burials carried out over many years went out of fashion as round barrows were established. These round barrows originally contained only one principal inhumation, the body being interred in the earth rather than laid on top of the ground. Secondary burials were frequently placed in the mound of earth, on occasion cutting into the primary inhumation.

Beaker culture: a name first used to describe a type of pottery vessel, shaped like a beaker, which started to appear in the late Neolithic and early Bronze Age. The name was then applied to the whole culture associated with this type of pottery, found predominantly in round barrows and other burials, and in some settlements. The pots display incised geometric decorations in parallel bands, and in burials it is usually found with other grave goods, mostly weapons such as arrowheads, wrist guards, and daggers. This may indicate the emergence of a ruling class of warriors in late Neolithic and early Bronze Age society.

Bluestone: a collective name for different kinds of stone from the Preseli hills in Wales, used for the shorter uprights at Stonehenge. The stones are blue or green inside when broken. See also dolerite and rhyolite.

Bronze Age: a title given to an era when the first metal tools and weapons start to appear, and part of a three-part nomenclature, Stone Age, Bronze Age, and Iron Age, invented to describe historical periods by the type of tools that were in general use. The date when metals appear in Britain has been revised and pushed further back in time to the mid-third millennium BC. There was no sharp temporal division between one culture and another and it is now thought that there was a much longer overlap between the late Neolithic and the Bronze Age than had been previously envisaged. Archaeologists now refer to this period by its initials LNEBA, late Neolithic/early Bronze Age, indicating the slow merger of the two cultures.

Causewayed enclosure: Neolithic monuments of the third millennium BC, defined by enclosing ditches and banks, sometimes up to three circuits, as at the type site at Windmill Hill. The ditches were on the outside and the banks thrown up on their inner edges, but the ditches were not continuous, being interrupted by causeways all around the monuments. The causewayed enclosures were not used at first as permanent settlements, but there is evidence from among the finds that people gathered maybe several times per year for feasting perhaps connected with rituals and ceremonials, or for exchange of gifts and trading activities. In their later history, some enclosures were converted into defensive areas, and excavations at one or two sites revealed signs of fighting before they were abandoned.

Cursus monument: long passageways, some of which ran for several miles, outlined by parallel banks and outer ditches, sometimes closed off at the ends and sometimes left open. The name was invented by William Stukeley after he had recognised the so-called Great Cursus north of Stonehenge. No one knows what function they fulfilled. Stukeley thought they must have been racetracks like the Roman circuses, and some authors have accepted this, with imaginative artwork showing people running. Others have suggested more macabre purposes, for the exposure of the dead until the flesh rotted away, the banks and ditches of the

Cursus monuments defining an area devoted to the dead, divided from the land of the living.

Dating techniques: these include dendrochronology, which utilises the annual growth layer of trees to pinpoint dates when timber was felled, and radiocarbon dating, which measures the decay of carbon-14 in bone and wood. Dendrochronology alone is less useful at Stonehenge, where remains of wooden posts and of implements are much less common than finds of animal and human bones of the Neolithic era, and antler picks, shoulder blade shovels and stone tools, which were often placed in ditches or under mounds, perhaps as offerings after the building work was completed. For establishing the age of materials such as these, archaeologists had to wait until the second half of the twentieth century, when radiocarbon dating was discovered by Willard Libby at the University of Chicago in 1949. In brief, all plants, animals and humans absorb radioactive carbon-14 from the atmosphere. Carbon-14 breaks down at a known rate. After 5,730 years have passed, the carbon-14 has diminished to only one half of its strength, referred to as its half-life. When any organism dies, carbon-14 stops being absorbed, so the measurement of the amount of carbon-14 left in bone or fragments of wood gives an indication of the age of the items. The dates established in this way can be compared to the dating evidence that has accumulated from dendrochronological studies, to produce a more accurate estimate of how old the finds are.

Dolerite: igneous rock, also called Bluestone, in consistency like basalt, but less finely grained than basalt. See also rhyolite.

Durrington Walls: henge monument only 2 miles from Stonehenge, and close to the River Avon in Wiltshire. The enclosure of about 11 acres is defined by a bank and inner ditch with entrances in the north-west and south-east. In its first phase Durrington Walls was probably contemporary with the first Stonehenge. At some unknown time after the bank and ditch was constructed, two circles of wooden posts were created inside the enclosure. Dating evidence from antler picks provides only a very broad range anywhere between the early to late third millennium BC. The northern circle in its first phase was 30 m across with an entrance to the south-west, but was replaced by another circle only half the size, with four large posts in the centre surrounded by rings of posts with an opening to the south. The southern circle also had two phases, the first with a diameter of 30 m, with four centre posts and an entrance to the south-east, which may have been protected by a porch. In the second phase this building was enlarged to 40 m, probably in the second half of the third millennium BC. These timber circles are usually portrayed in reconstruction drawings as roofed buildings, but could have been open circles of free-standing posts. This is how the reconstruction of the southern circle was built by the Time Team at Upavon in Wiltshire. The northern circle may have been a house, while the southern circle provided a cult house, but this is not certain. House floors have been found outside the henge, to the north of the processional way or Avenue leading from the south-east entrance to the River Avon.

Flint: nodules of flint are found in cretaceous chalk. Prehistoric people went to great lengths to obtain flint to make weapons and tools, illustrated by the extensive galleries that were constructed at Grimes Graves in Norfolk, where flint was extracted by mining. All kinds of tools can be made from flint by striking it with another stone. When chipped it forms flakes which can be ground down to make sharp edges. Flint was used for a wide range of tools, from tiny arrowheads to handheld scrapers and larger axes.

Hawkins, Gerald S. English-born scientist who became Chairman of the Department of Astronomy at the University of Boston, and worked in association with the Smithsonian Astrophysical Observatory at Cambridge, Massachusetts. He examined the alignments of Stonehenge and suggested that it had been developed far beyond its use as a solar and lunar observatory, encompassing a wealth of astronomical alignments to various stars. Many archaeologists have strongly disputed his theories, but interest in his work has not been obliterated and his ideas keep on turning up in books, so the astronomical ideas have been discredited but not disproved.

Henge: these Neolithic monuments are distinguished by shape and design, usually a roughly circular enclosure defined by a bank of earth with an interior ditch. They vary in size and in their internal features, but often contained circles of wooden posts or of stones, sometimes more than one. They were probably ceremonial centres, perhaps taking over the functions of the causewayed enclosures as meeting places for festivals, trading and gift exchange, and religious ceremonies. Some henges contain burials or cremated bone, and pits where rubbish was buried, often indicating that feasts had been held. Modern archaeologist Thomas Kendrick invented the term 'henge' in 1932, on analogy with Stonehenge itself, despite the fact that it does not actually fit the strict definition of a henge monument, having its ditch outside the bank. The ceremonials carried out there were probably the same as those at other henges.

Megalithic: a term derived from ancient Greek, literally meaning large stones. It does not define a period of prehistory like Neolithic or Mesolithic, but is applied to any kind of monument which uses large stones, such as single standing stones, stone circles or tombs with compartments defined by huge stones.

Mesolithic: Middle Stone Age, from the ancient Greek *meso* (middle) and *lithos* (stone).

Neolithic: New Stone Age, from the Greek *neo* (new) and *lithos* (stone). This long period of prehistory was distinguished from its predecessors, the Palaeolithic and Mesolithic, by the gradual introduction of stone tools in addition to flint, and the domestication of animals and the development of farming.

Palaeolithic: the very earliest prehistoric era, usually divided by archaeologists into lower, middle, and upper Palaeolithic to define various cultures of the hunter-gatherers, from the races preceding *Homo sapiens*, through Neanderthal people to hunters of the Ice Age.

Post hole: when a wooden post or a stone has been sunk into the earth and has since disappeared, the profile of the hole can usually be discovered by excavation, because the soil that fills the hole is often darker than the surrounding ground. Archaeologists can usually distinguish between deliberate backfilling of a hole and a gradual process as the sides collapse and soil accumulates.

Q and R holes: two concentric rings of holes preceding the Sarsen Circle and the Trilithons at Stonehenge. Fragments of Bluestone were found in the holes, so it is assumed that they held a double ring of these stones, but there was no excavation on the east side of the circle so it is possible to argue that this circle was planned but never completed, or that it was only ever intended to build a half-circle. The Q and R holes are therefore related to the Bluestone controversy, and the debate about how they arrived at Stonehenge from south-west Wales.

Radiocarbon dating: see dating techniques.

Rhyolite: fine-grained acid igneous rock, also called Bluestone, often formed from volcanic ash flowing in high temperature gas clouds. See also dolerite.

Sarsen: very hard sandstone, only slightly less hard than steel. The name is thought to derive from 'sazzan', an old Wiltshire term which may be related to 'sasan', an Indian word for burial grounds. The Anglo-Saxon term was 'sar-stan' meaning hard stone, with connotations of toughness and also difficulty in shaping them.

Stukeley, William (1687–1765): in the 1720s Stukeley began to study the landscape of Stonehenge, and he continued to do so for four more seasons, discovering the Avenue leading from the north-east entrance, and the Great Cursus to the north. He also noted the alignment to the midsummer sunrise, but, having little to support his studies except the classical authors, he was convinced that the monument belonged to the Druids. He made several detailed plans and drawings of the monuments he examined and surveyed, and his admirable work was published. No one can study Stonehenge without referring to his work, not least because his drawings show the state of the monument in his day, since when some stones have fallen down or been removed.

Trilithon: William Stukeley invented this term, meaning 'three stones' for the five separate structures of the Horseshoe in the middle of Stonehenge, each consisting of two large uprights and a lintel.

West Kennet Barrow: tomb near Windmill Hill, used throughout the Neolithic and early Bronze Age.

Windmill Hill: situated on high ground near Avebury, Windmill Hill has become the type site for causewayed enclosures. It covered nearly 21 acres, and was surrounded by three widely spaced concentric rings of ditches with frequent causeways across them. Activity on the site preceded the building of the enclosure. The outer ditch cut into shallow trenches forming the sides of a square, with pits inside it, which may have been a mortuary house for the dead before interment. Several kinds of pottery were found at Windmill Hill, including types originating from areas some distance from the monument, so it is thought that it acted as a distribution centre. There seems to have been no permanent settlement within the enclosure, but people visited and stayed for extended periods. No definite evidence for houses has been found but scatters of flints on the slopes of the hill outside the enclosure may indicate settlement sites. The site went out of use in the Neolithic period, perhaps replaced by Avebury. The finds, especially the pottery, form the basis of the Windmill Hill culture named after the site.

Woodhenge: this henge monument is just over 6 miles from Stonehenge, close to the larger henge at Durrington Walls. It is small, only about 15 feet across the circle, which was almost completely filled by six concentric rings of post holes which had held wooden posts. The structure is variously interpreted as a circular building, with a sloping roof with a hole at the top, or simply as six circles of free-standing posts. Neither interpretation prevents its suggested use for ritual or cult purposes, which is emphasised by the discovery of a grave in the centre of the post circles, containing the body of a child whose skull had been cleft in two.

Y and Z holes: two concentric lines of holes surrounding the Sarsen Circle at Stonehenge, the last to be created at the monument, the Z holes at the end of the third millennium BC and the Y holes possibly in the middle of the second millennium. The holes were perhaps meant to echo the thirty stones of the Sarsen ring but were never properly finished, and they probably never held posts or stones.

FURTHER READING

Burl, A. 1981. *Rites of the Gods*. Dent.

Burl, A. 2007. *Stonehenge: a complete history and archaeology of the world's most enigmatic stone circle*. Constable & Robinson Ltd.

Castleden, R. 1993. *The Making of Stonehenge*. Routledge.

Chippindale, C. 1994. *Stonehenge Complete*. Thames & Hudson. Revised edition.

Cleal, R., Walker, K. E., and Montague. R. (eds.) 1995. *Stonehenge in its Landscape: twentieth-century excavations*. English Heritage.

Darvill, T. 1987. *Prehistoric Britain*. Reprinted 2003. Routledge.

Darvill, T. 2007. *Stonehenge: the biography of a landscape*. Tempus.

John, B. 2008. *The Bluestone Enigma: Stonehenge, Preseli and the Ice Age*. Greencroft Books.

Lewis-Williams, D. and Pearce, D. 2005. *Inside the Neolithic Mind: consciousness, cosmos and the realm of the gods*. Thames & Hudson.

Malone, C. 1989. *Avebury*. Batsford/English Heritage.

McClintock, J. 2006. *The Stonehenge Companion*. English Heritage.

North, J. 1996. *Stonehenge: Neolithic man and the cosmos*. HarperCollins.

Pollard, J. 2002. *Neolithic*. Shire Books.

Pryor, F. 2004. *Britain BC*. Harper Perennial.

ABOUT THE AUTHOR

Patricia Southern is an authority on the early history of England and Europe and the author of thirteen history books and historical biographies, including *Roman Britain: A New History* ('A comprehensive and accessible history of Roman Britain' *BRITISH MUSEUM MAGAZINE*). She lives in Northumberland.

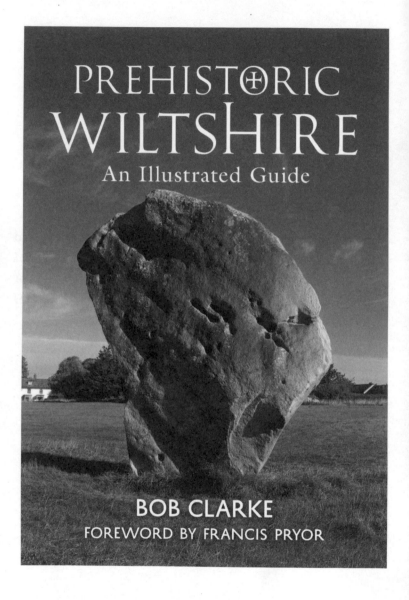

PREHIST⊕RIC
WILTSHIRE
An Illustrated Guide

BOB CLARKE
FOREWORD BY FRANCIS PRYOR